© Copyright 2015 Douglas Snipp

This book, it's author, and it's publisher are
not associated with, endorsed by, or sponsored by Roblox Corporation.
ROBLOX ® is a registered trademark of Roblox Corporation.

ROBLOX LUA: SCRIPTING FOR BEGINNERS

TABLE OF CONTENTS

1	**INTRODUCTION**
2	**ROBLOX STUDIO**
2	Setting up ROBLOX Studio
7	Parts and Tools
13	Adding Teams and Spawns
18	Challenge
20	**THE VERY BASICS**
20	Parents and Children
21	How to add a Script Object
23	Variables
24	Making Variables as Objects
25	Printing Variables
26	Creating Variables with script
28	Challenge
29	**FUNCTIONS AND EVENTS**
29	Writing a function
30	Calling functions and using Events
33	Using debounce
35	Another way to write functions
36	Challenge
37	**MORE ON SCRIPTING**
37	Script Object's location
39	Shortcuts in scripts
41	**GUIs**
41	What is a GUI?
43	Objects we can put inside GUIs
45	Properties of GUI Objects
48	Scripting our GUI
51	**LEADERBOARD SCRIPT-THROUGH**
51	Introduction to script-through
52	Creating the Leaderboard
54	Scripting a coin that gives Points
56	Players, Characters, Humanoids
57	Increasing Deaths when a player dies
60	**GUI TELEPORTER SCRIPT-THROUGH**
60	Introduction to script-through
61	Making our GUI
63	Scripting the teleport
64	**TOOL GIVER SCRIPT-THROUGH**
64	Introduction to script-through
64	Making the Invisibility Tool
68	Scripting the Giver Brick
71	**WHAT NOW?**

INTRODUCTION

Welcome to ROBLOX Lua for beginners. With this book, I'm going to introduce you to the ideas you need to be able to understand in order make your own scripts and to make your own games. This book will not teach you how script every single thing possible in ROBLOX. Instead, you should learn how scripts work and are made, so that you can make your own.

First, we'll take a look at how to set up and use ROBLOX Studio, then we will take a look at the basics of scripting and go through a few examples. By the end of the book, you will be able to turn your ideas for games into reality.

ROBLOX STUDIO
SETTING UP ROBLOX STUDIO

Before we can learn how to script, we need to become familiar with ROBLOX Studio. Being able to use Studio easily is really important, so don't skip this step. First, we are going to learn how to set up the View for scripting and get a good understanding of what some of the buttons and options in Studio are used for.

Let's make a new Place:
1. Click "File".
2. Click "New".

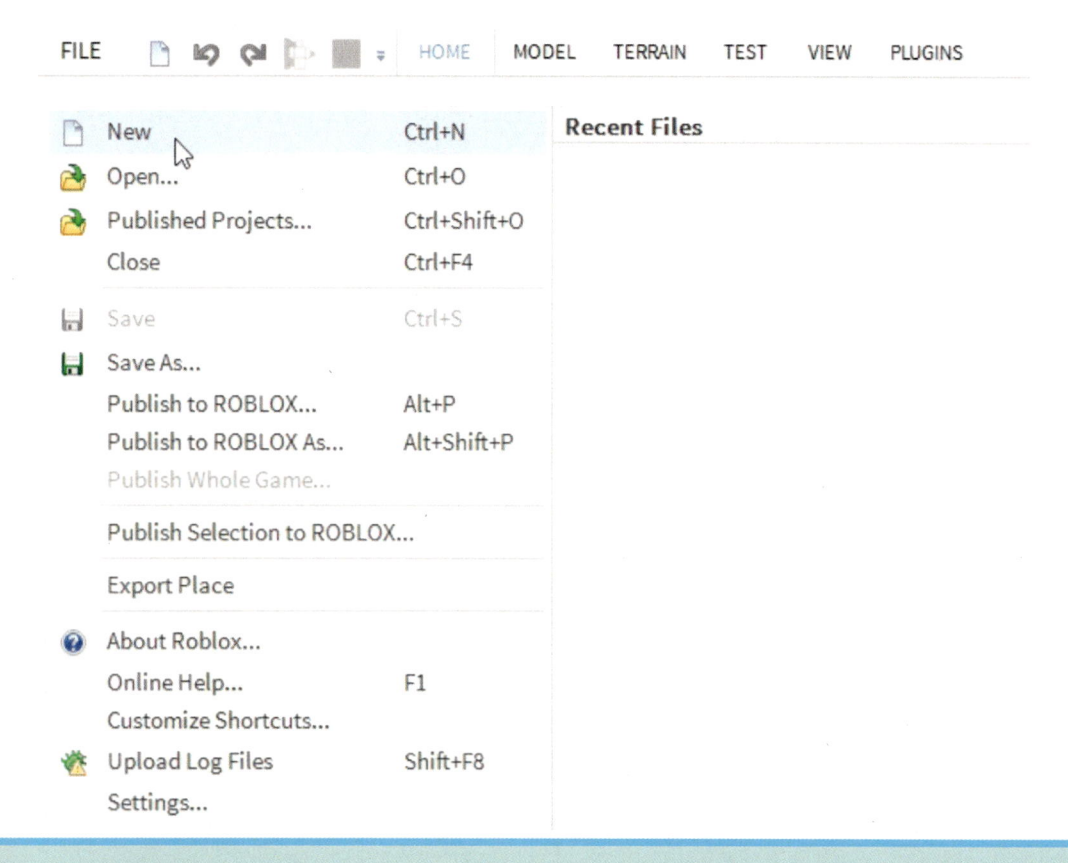

NIFTY NUGGET: You can press the Ctrl key and N at the same time to make a new Place, too.

Now, we need to set up Studio so we can easily edit our game.
1. Click on the "View" tab at the top of the screen.
2. The 3 windows we need to use often are "Output", "Properties" and "Explorer". Click on these buttons so that they're the only ones highlighted.

ROBLOX STUDIO

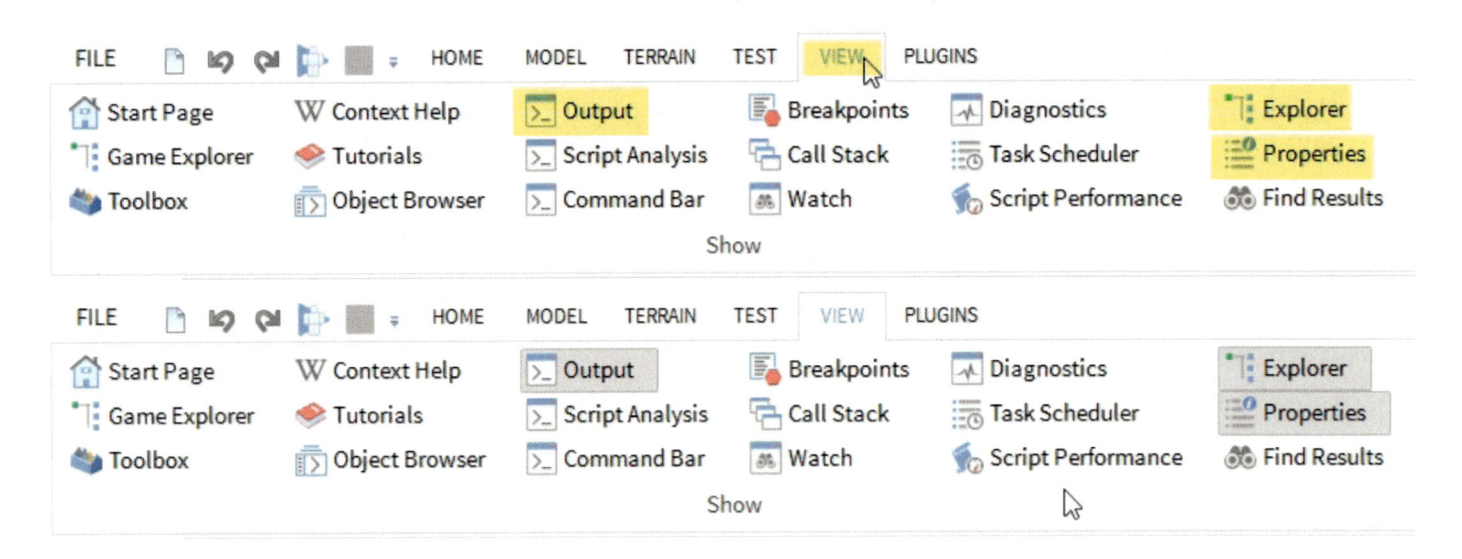

3. You can click and drag the grey bar at the top of the window to move the window around the screen. I suggest setting up your screen to look like mine.

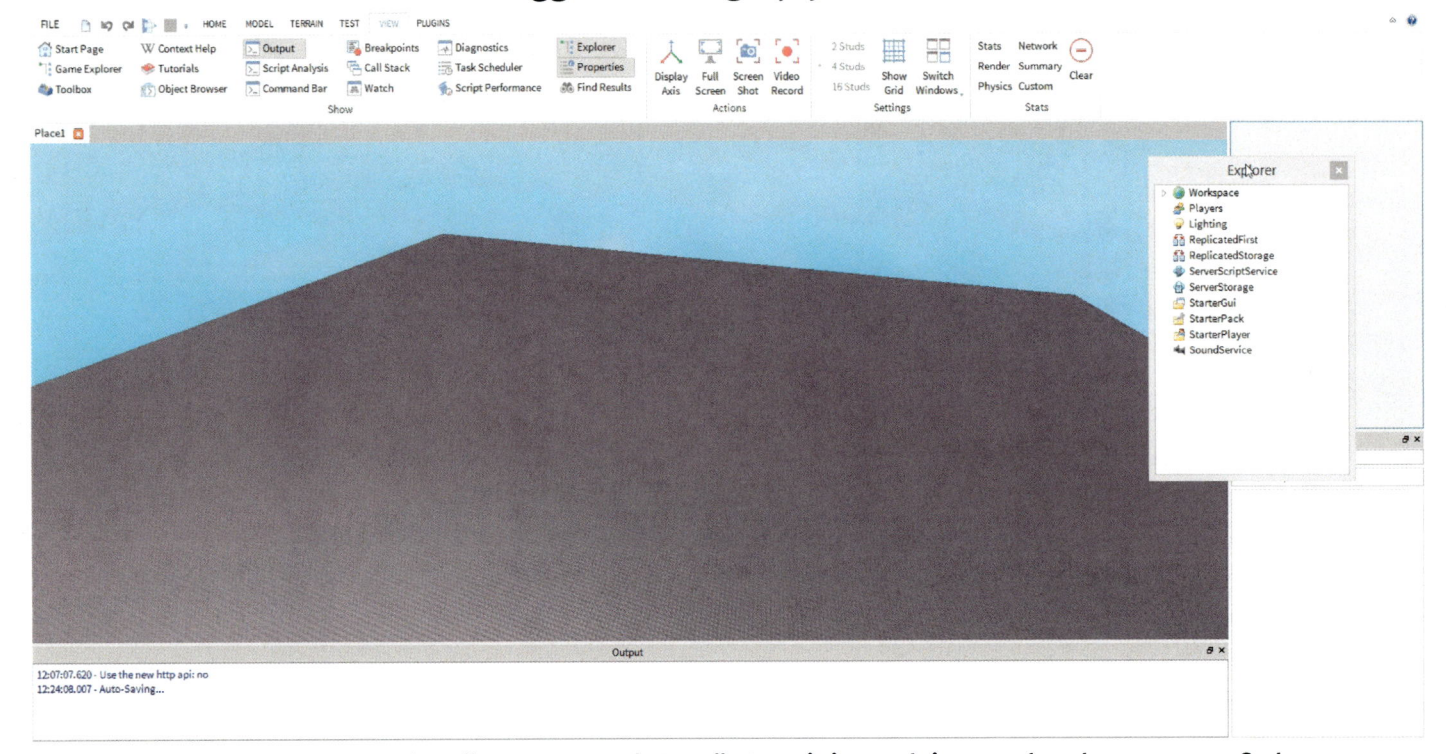

4. Next, open the "Command Bar". Position this at the bottom of the screen, underneath "Output".

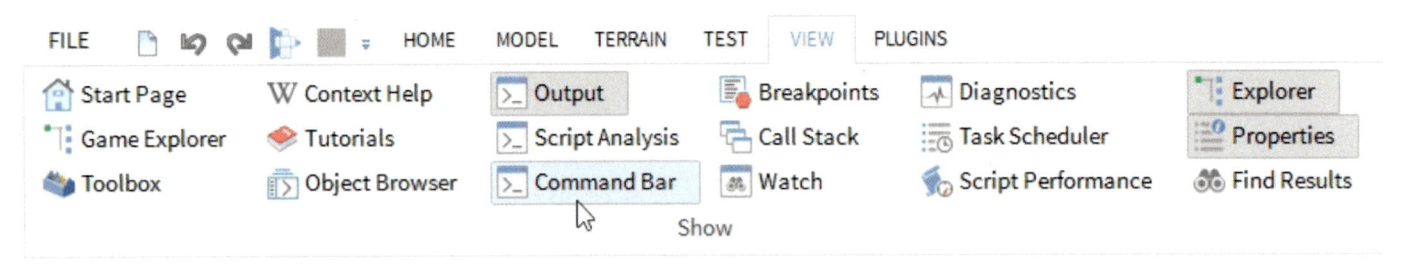

ROBLOX LUA: SCRIPTING FOR BEGINNERS

5.   From time to time, we will also be using the "Toolbox" window, which you can find under the "View" tab, and the "Advanced Objects" window, which is under the "Model" tab.

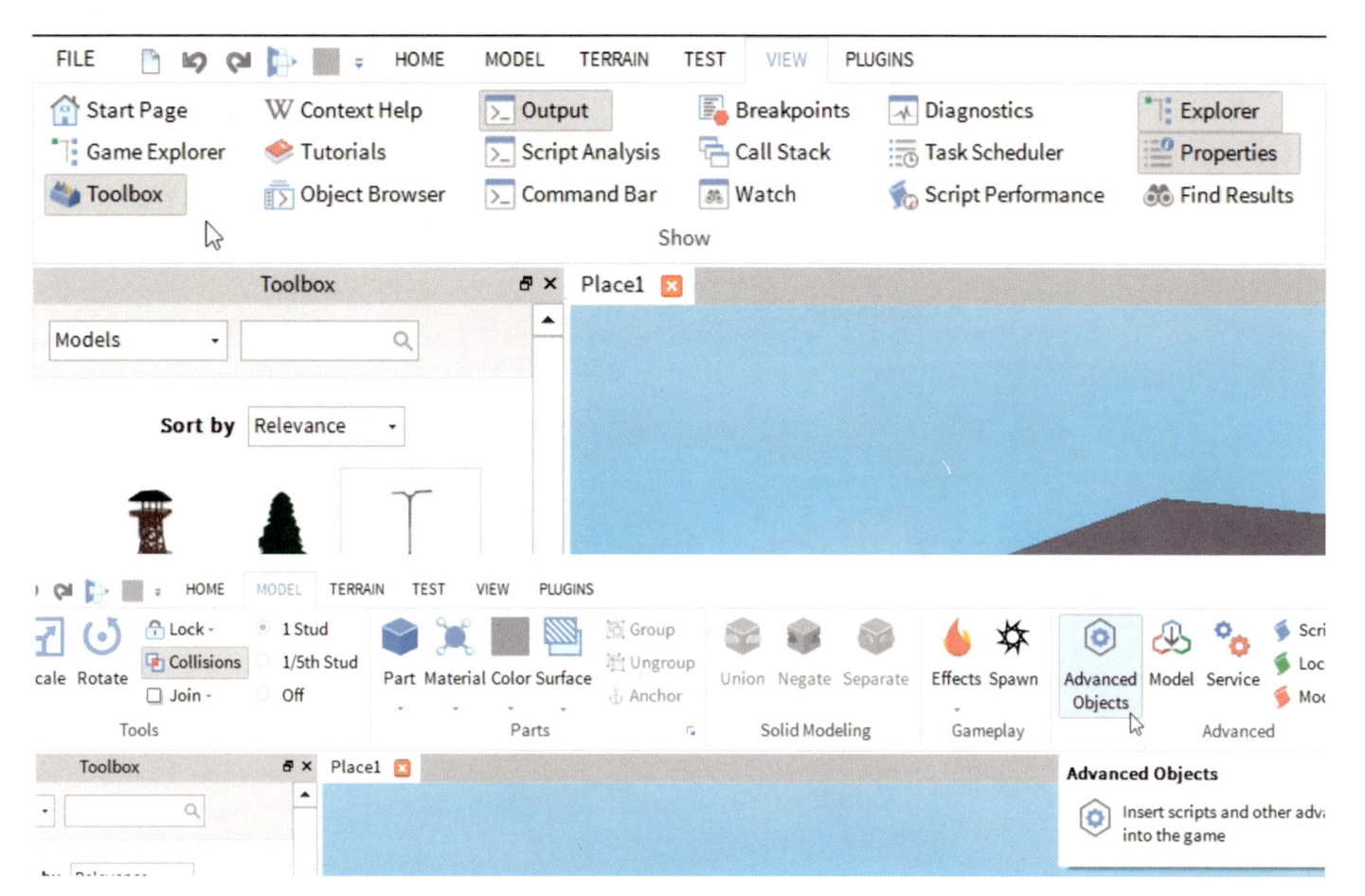

Take a read through these boxes. They will show you what each of these windows does.

EXPLORER

The Explorer shows you absolutely everything that makes up your game. The most important section for now is "Workspace". Press the small arrow (pictured) to see all of the Parts in your game.

The Workspace section is where new Parts go when you add them. Now click on "BasePlate". This lets you select the big grey brick that is there whenever you make a new game.

ROBLOX STUDIO

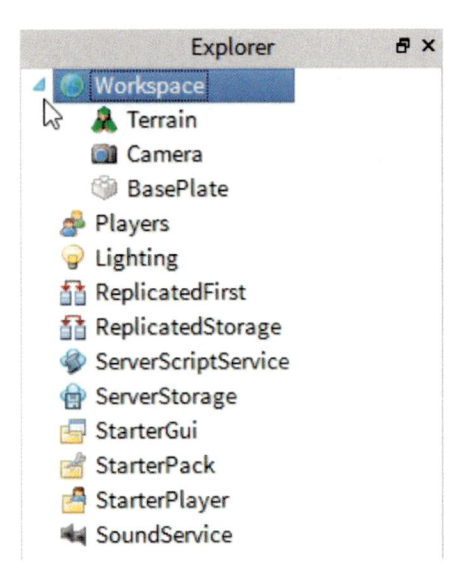

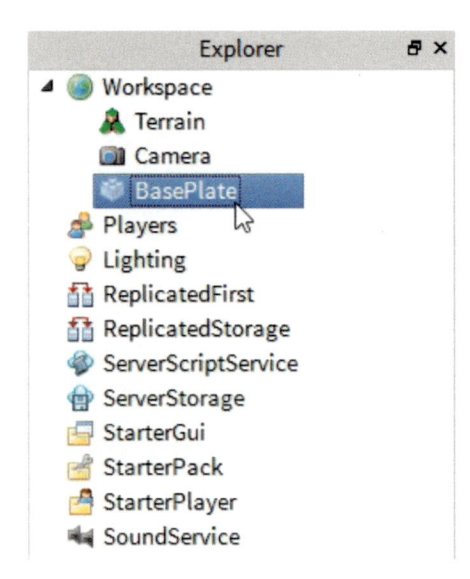

PROPERTIES

Properties will show you all of the details about any Part that is selected. For example, "BrickColor". Try clicking on "BrickColor" and changing it. Other important details about Parts in the Properties window include the Part's name, size and position.

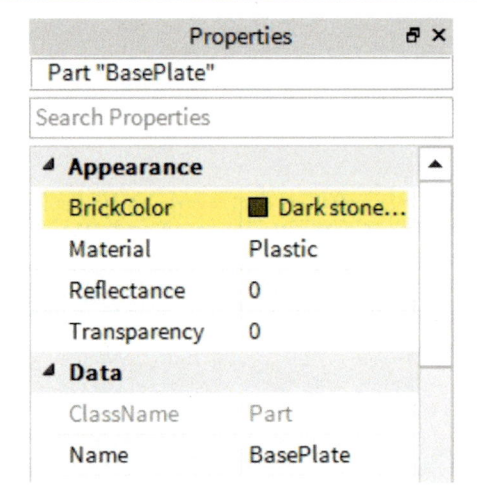

OUTPUT

The output window will show you if there are any mistakes in your script. You can also use script to make text come up in the Output box, which we will learn how to do later.

ROBLOX LUA: SCRIPTING FOR BEGINNERS

COMMAND BAR

The command bar lets you type in a single line of script while you are testing your game. This can be useful for checking your script while playing.

TOOLBAR

In the Toolbox, you can browse through Models and Decals made by you, other players and ROBLOX. There are some useful things in here, for example the scripts in the "ROBLOX Sets" section. You can search for Models made by other players to insert them into your game – these can be really useful to learn scripting from, because you can take a look at how other players have scripted the things you are trying to do.

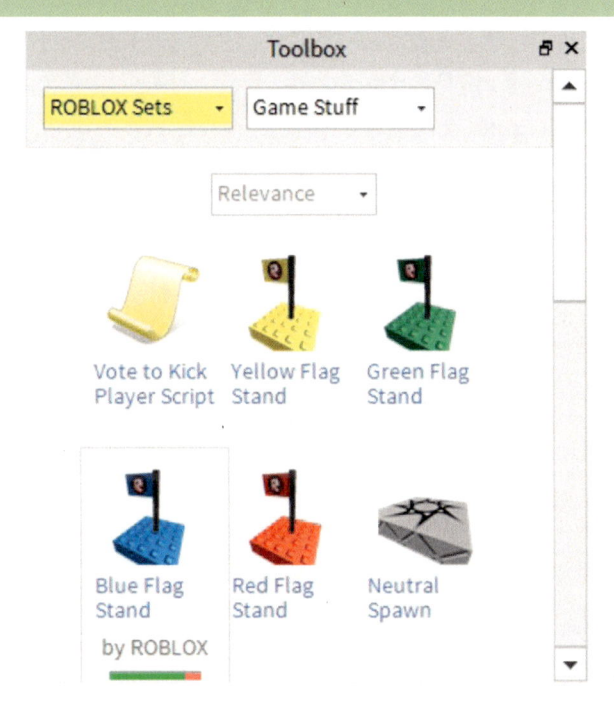

ADVANCED OBJECTS

Advanced Objects brings up a number of different items that you can insert into the Workspace and other Explorer sections. We'll be using some of these later on.

ROBLOX STUDIO

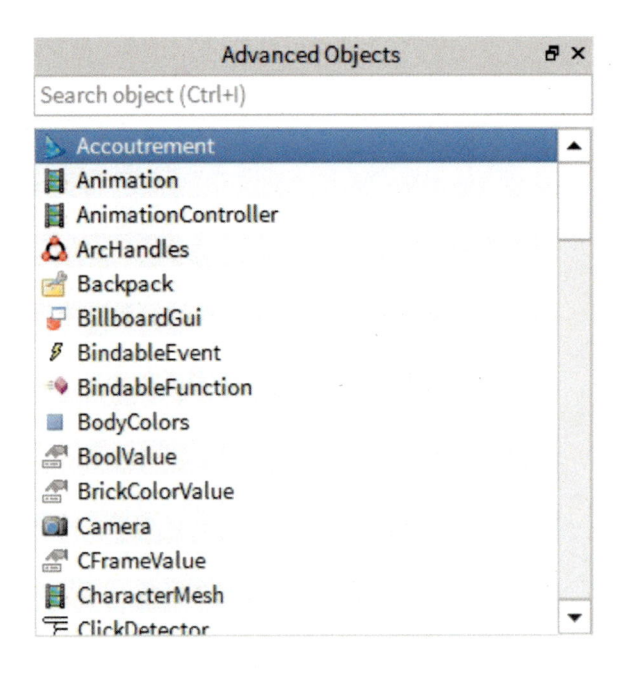

PARTS AND TOOLS

To add a new Part, right-click on Workspace and select "Insert Part" from the drop-down menu. You can also insert Parts from the "Home" tab – there are some more options here as you can also add spheres, wedges or cylinders.

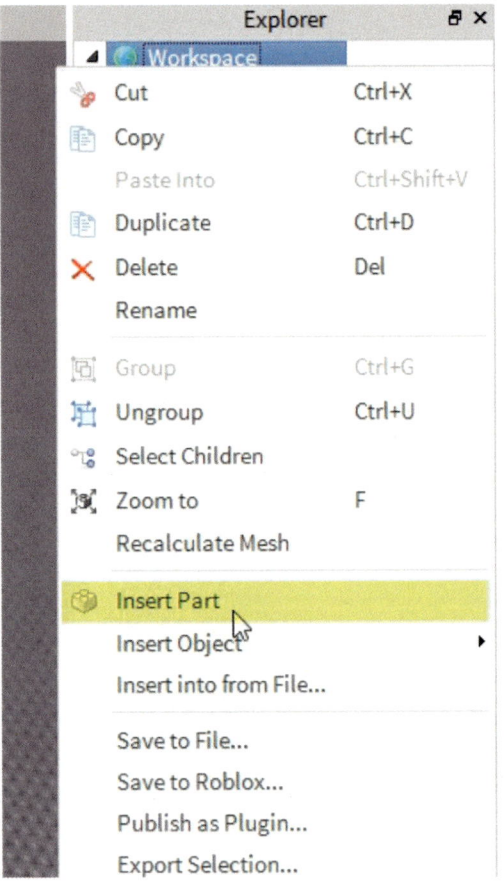

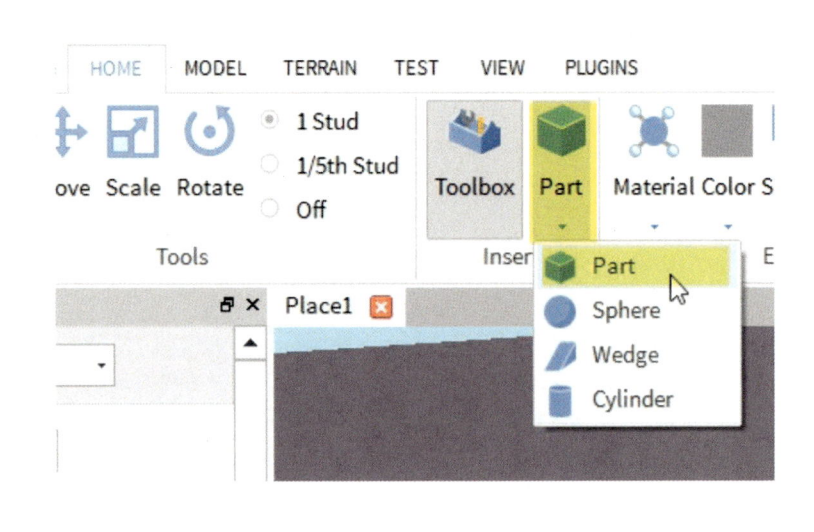

Click on "Part" under Workspace to be able to access it's Properties. Let's change the Part's Name:
1. Select the Part so that it is highlighted in blue in the Workspace.
2. Go to the Properties window.

3. Scroll down the Properties window to the "Data" section where you will see Name.
4. Click on where it says "Part" and then type in any name you want. I've used "brick".

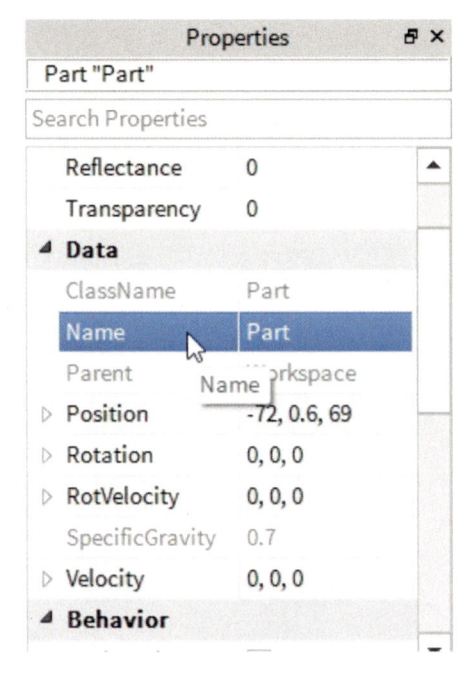

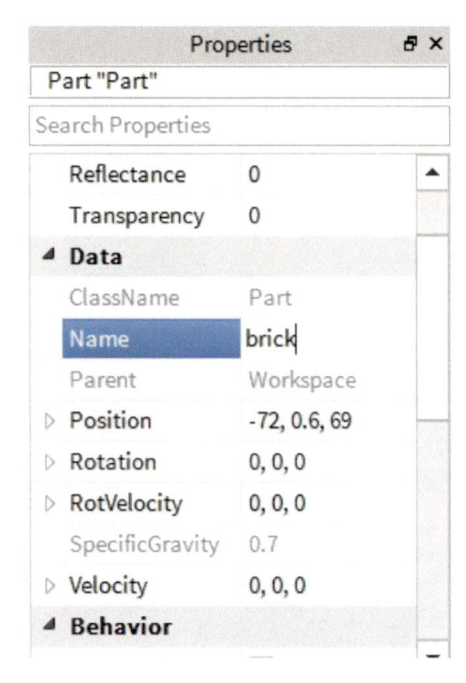

ROBLOX STUDIO

The name of the Part has now changed in the Workspace, too. You should give important Parts names when you are making your game – this will help you find them when you have thousands of bricks in the Workspace!

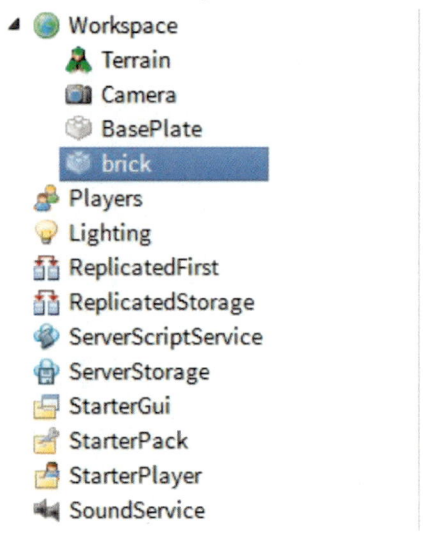

Now let's take a look at the tools we will using in Studio to edit Parts. Click on the "Home" tab. Take a read through these boxes to get an idea of what each tool does.

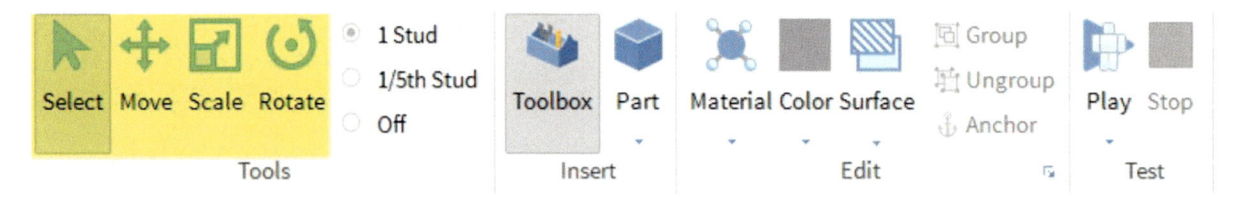

SELECT

You can use the Select tool to pick out Parts in your game. Clicking on something when you are using the Select tool will highlight it in the Workspace.

NIFTY NUGGET: "Locked" objects cannot be selected with the Select Tool. Try selecting the BasePlate – it doesn't work. To unlock the BasePlate, click the BasePlate in the Workspace and go to Properties. Scroll down to where it says "Locked" and uncheck the box.

MOVE

Selecting the Move tool and then clicking on a Part allows you to move the Part in one direction by clicking and dragging the arrows. This can be useful when you need to move a Part by just one or two Studs or when you're trying to get a big Part in a specific place.

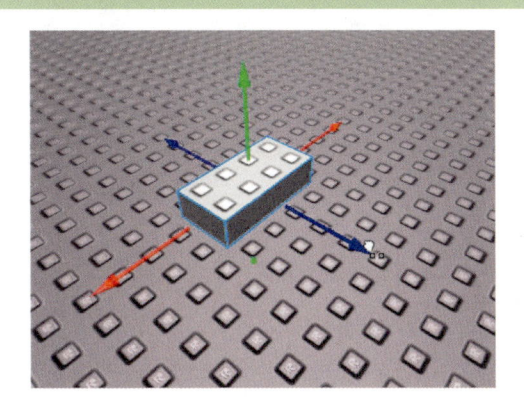

SCALE

Scale will allow you to change the size of Parts. Clicking one of the circles and dragging will scale the Part in that direction only.

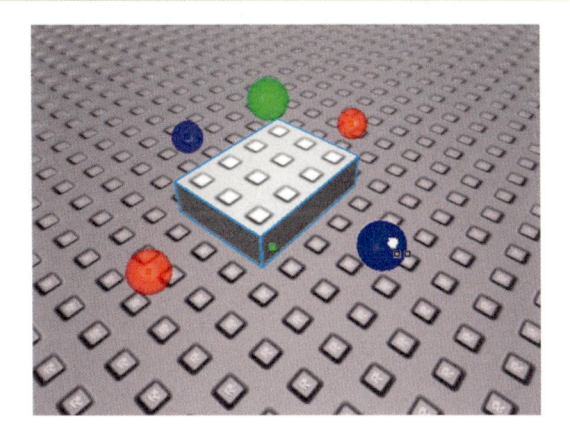

ROTATE

With Rotate, you can spin a Part in any direction. Again, just select a circle and drag it to rotate the Part.

ROBLOX STUDIO

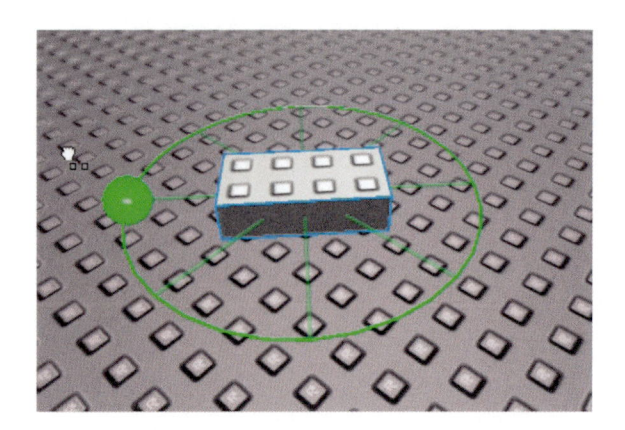

STUD SIZE

Try selecting the different Stud sizes and Scale the Part. With "1 Stud" selected, you can only Scale, Move and Rotate the Part in big jumps. "1/5 Stud" allows smaller jumps, and with "Off" you can Scale the Part to any size. Try playing with these settings to understand what they do. I would recommend that you stick to 1 Stud most of the time. Using 1 Stud makes building much easier and quicker.

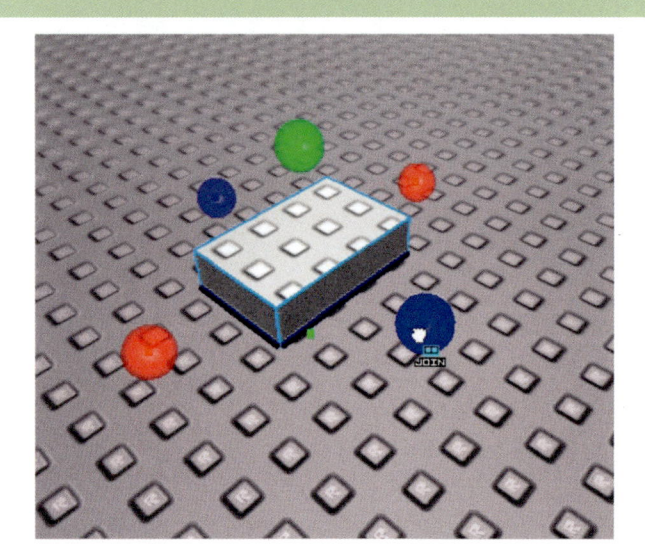

ANCHOR

If a Part has "Anchor" turned on, this means that a player cannot move the Part by walking into it, and that if you put the Part in the air, it will stay in the air without dropping to the ground when you test the game.

ROBLOX LUA: SCRIPTING FOR BEGINNERS

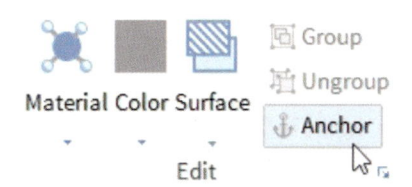

The Anchor Tool is under the "Home" tab.

This is a brick with Anchor turned on. It can float in the air.

This is the same brick with Anchor turned off. It has fallen onto the ground.

PLAY

To test your game, click the Play button. When you're done testing your game, press the Stop button.

ROBLOX STUDIO

MATERIAL, COLOR AND SURFACE

You can use these buttons to change what the Part looks like. If a Part has "Anchor" turned off, using a different Surface will change how strongly that Part is held to another Part, and different Surfaces will make it harder to move the Part. For example: if a "Weld" surface is touching another brick's "Weld" surface, it will be very hard to break the two bricks apart.

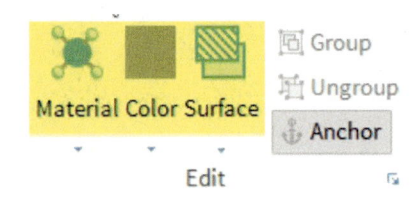

That covers all of the basics we need to understand in Studio for now. Next, let's set up a Team and Spawn location for our game to get more familiar with Studio.

ADDING TEAMS AND SPAWNS

Understanding how to use Teams and being able to set your own Spawn location will give you much better control over your game. This is also a good way to practice using the features of Studio, which we've taken a look at in the last section.

> **NIFTY NUGGET:** Spawns are Parts which you stand on when you start the game, or when you die and respawn. You can use Teams to spawn in a different place, or if you want to make a game where one team plays against another.

To add a Spawn Location:
1. Open up the Toolbox.
2. Go into ROBLOX Sets, and then "Game Stuff".
3. Click on "Neutral Spawn".
4. Position the Spawn Location somewhere on the BasePlate.

ROBLOX LUA: SCRIPTING FOR BEGINNERS

Okay, so now we have made a Spawn Location, and your character will start here when you press Play. But what happens if we want to add another Spawn, or to add Teams which players can join? To do this, we need to add the Teams Service:

1. Go to the "Model" tab and click "Service".
2. Click "Teams" then press Insert.
3. The Teams folder will now appear in the Explorer.

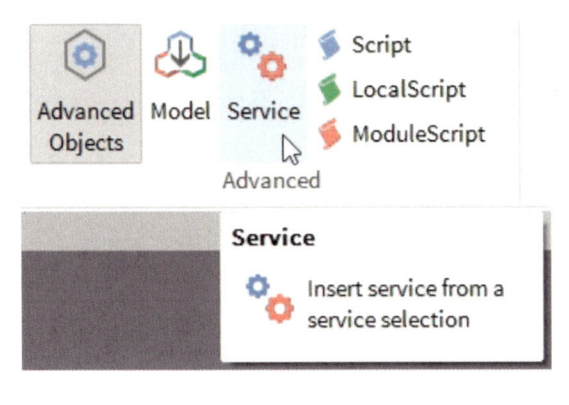

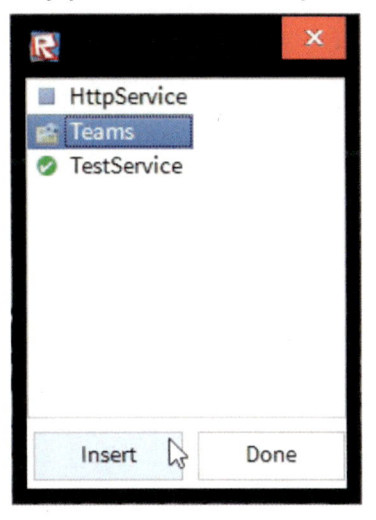

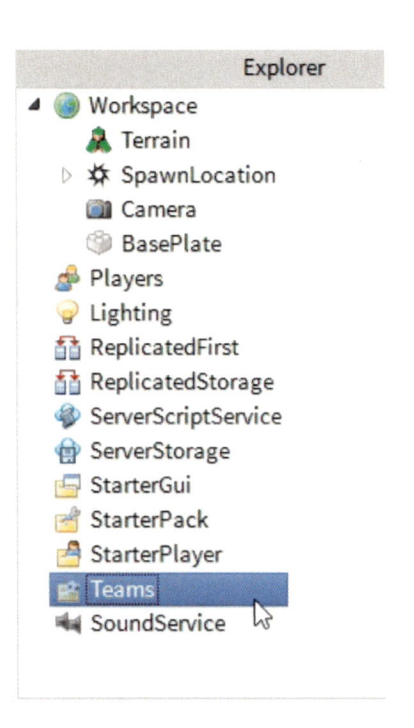

ROBLOX STUDIO

Now, we are going to add a new Team:
1. Open the Advanced Objects window.
2. Double-click "Team".
3. The new Team will now appear in the Teams folder in the Explorer.

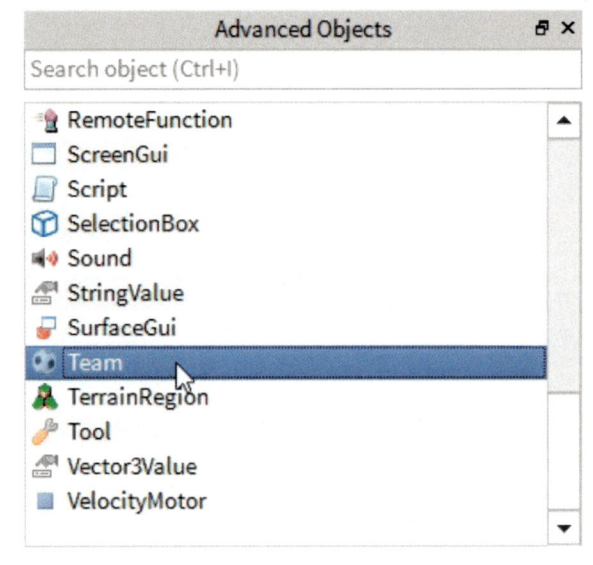

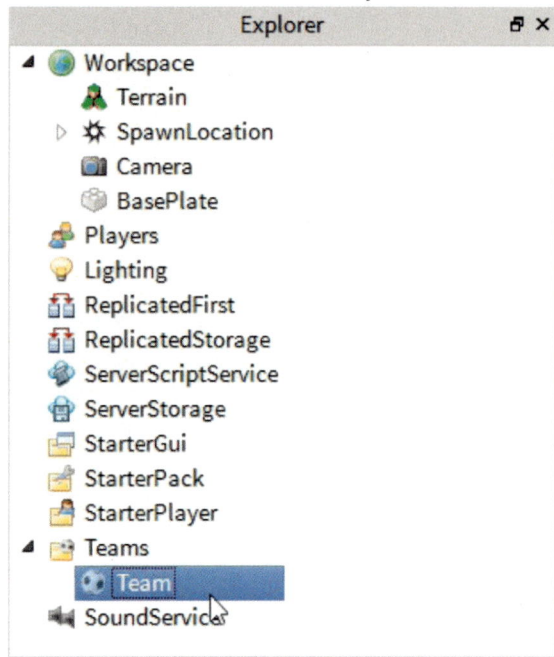

Click the Team in the Explorer and take a look at it's Properties. We can change the Name of the team here. Let's call it "Blue Team". There is another property called "TeamColor". "TeamColor" is found when you press the Team in the Explorer. Let's make our team's color be "Really Blue". TeamColor is also found when you press the Spawn Location in the Explorer and look at it's Properties.

The two TeamColors on a Spawn and in a Team need to match if you want the Spawn to be used by that team.

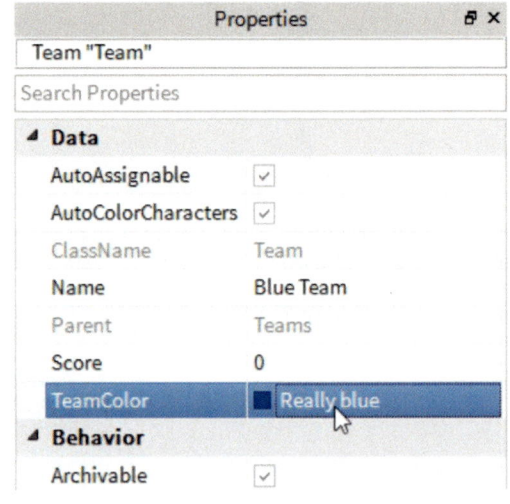

TeamColor of Team 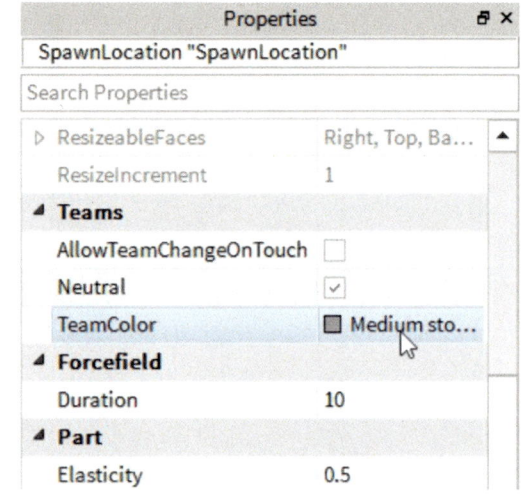   *TeamColor of SpawnLocation*

When you select Team, there is another property that says "Auto-Assignable". If this is checked, any player that joins the game can be put into this team. If this is unchecked, the only way to join the team is to stand on that team's Spawn. Uncheck the "Auto-Assignable" property for this team.

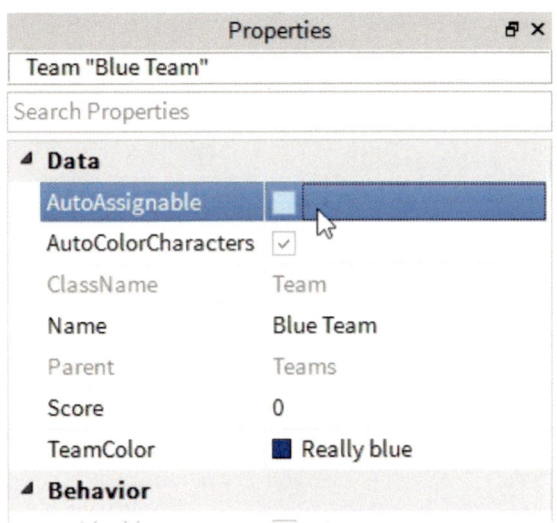

Press Play.

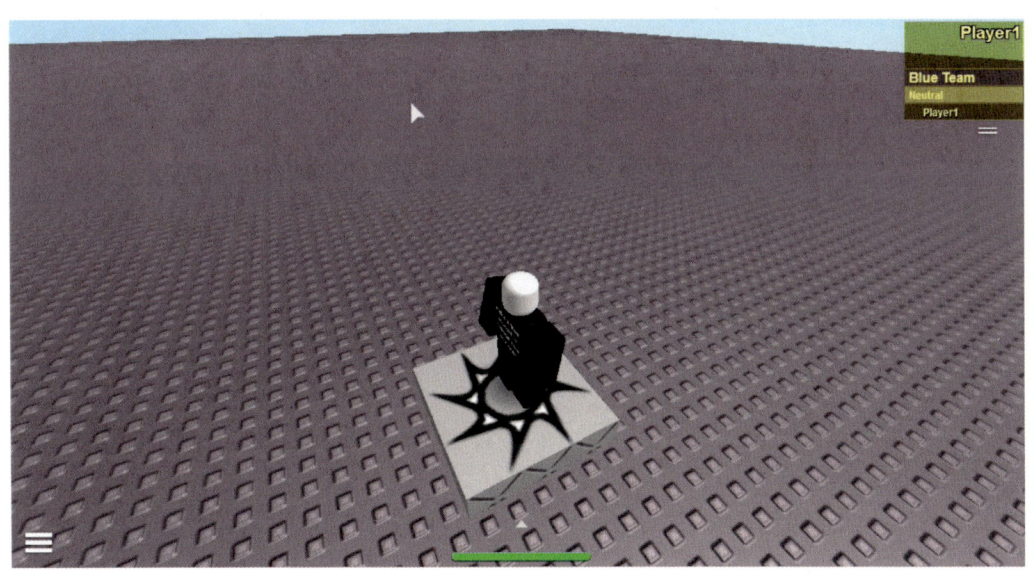

Your character will be standing on the Spawn, and if you look at the top right-hand corner, the character will be in the "Neutral" team. Note: "Neutral" is **not** actually a Team. A player is in "Neutral" when they're not in any team. How do we let the player join the Blue Team?

1. Add another Neutral Spawn from the Toolbox.
2. Click the new Spawn using the Select Tool, so that it's highlighted in the Explorer.

ROBLOX STUDIO

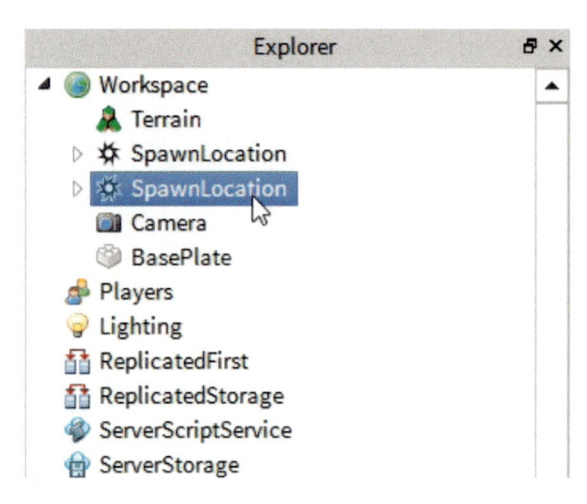

3. Go to the Properties window and scroll down to "TeamColor". Change it to "Really Blue".

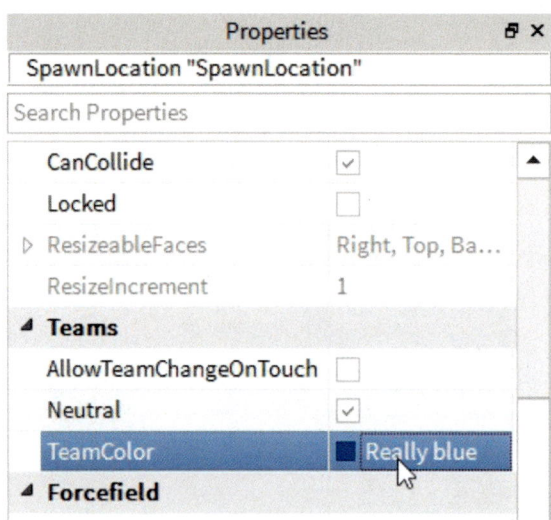

4. To let players join this team when they step on the Spawn, we need to check the "AllowTeamChangeOnTouch" box.

5. We also need to uncheck the "Neutral" box.

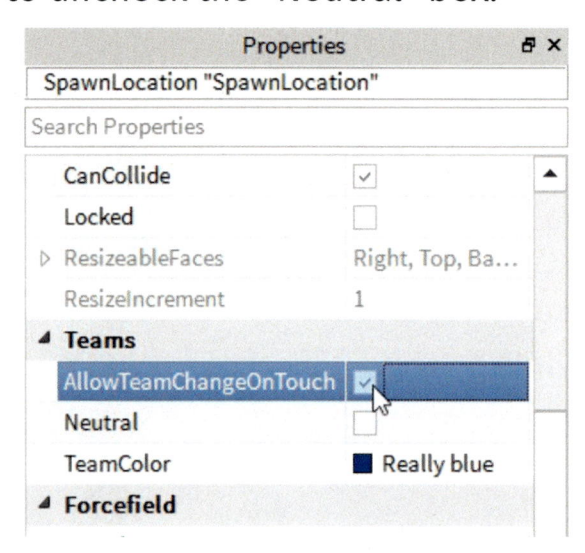

Press Play and test it out.
To make it more obvious which Spawn belongs to the Blue Team, we can go to Brick-Color in the Spawn Location's Properties and change it to "Really Blue".

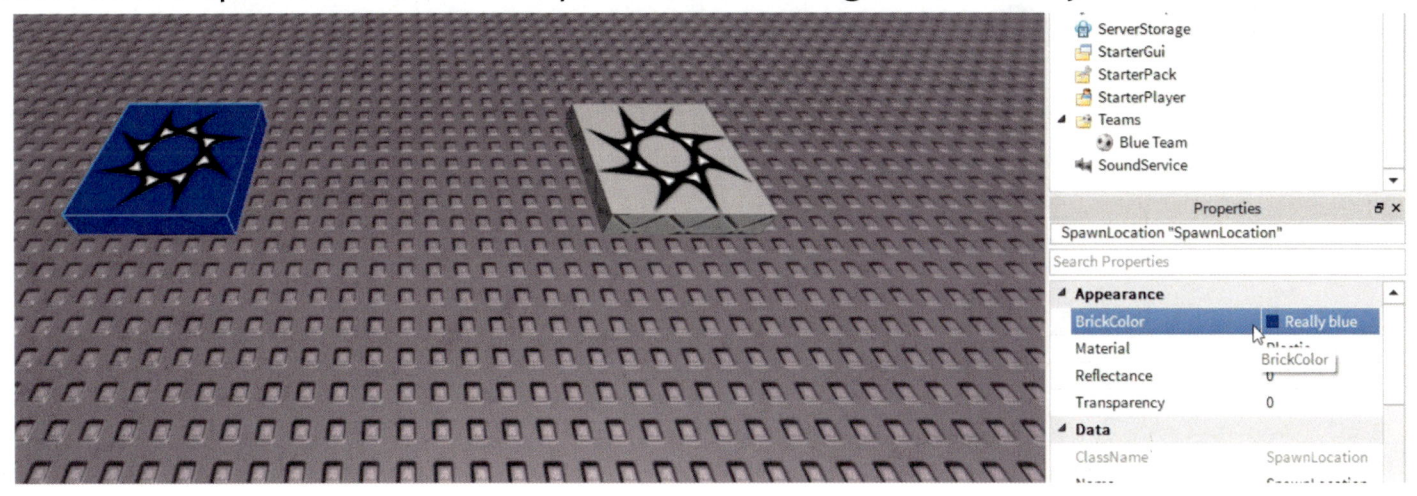

Now, when we join the Blue Team, "Neutral" will disappear and we can't rejoin it by standing on the grey Spawn. Like I mentioned above, this is because there is no such thing as the "Neutral" team. This brings you to your first Challenge:

CHALLENGE

Your challenge is to add a Yellow Team and a Yellow Spawn. Right now, you have one blue Spawn and one grey Spawn. I want you to:
    1.   Add a new Team, name it "Yellow Team", and change it's TeamColor to "New Yeller". Turn "Auto-Assignable" off.
    2.   Change the TeamColor of the grey Spawn to "New Yeller".
    3.   Change the BrickColor of the grey Spawn to "New Yeller".
    4.   Change the Name of the yellow Spawn to "Yellow Spawn" in the Properties.
    5.   When you step onto the Yellow Spawn, your character should be put into the "Yellow Team", and when you step on the blue Spawn, your character should be put into the "Blue Team".

Having trouble? Think about...
- Do your TeamColors match?
- Have you turned "AllowTeamChangeOnTouch" on to let your character join this team when they walk on the Yellow Spawn?
- Have you turned "Neutral" off?

ROBLOX STUDIO

NIFTY NUGGET: Your character is automatically put into "Neutral" when you test the game. If you want to add a Team for new players, make one and set "Auto-Assignable" to on by checking the box, and call it something like "Undecided". This means that all players who haven't touched a Spawn yet will be put into the Undecided team.

THE VERY BASICS

PARENTS AND CHILDREN

In ROBLOX Studio, objects in the Explorer are classed as "Parents" and "Children":
- The **Child** of "brick" is "Script".
- The **Parent** of "brick" is "Workspace".

When one object is inside another in the Explorer (like how the Script is inside "brick"), it is a **Child** inside a **Parent**.

It can be helpful to think of Parents and Children as a tree and it's branches

THE VERY BASICS

In this picture:
- What is the Parent of "Script Two"?
- What is the Child of "Square"?
- What is the Parent of "Square"?

This is very important to understand for scripting, and we will use it all the time.

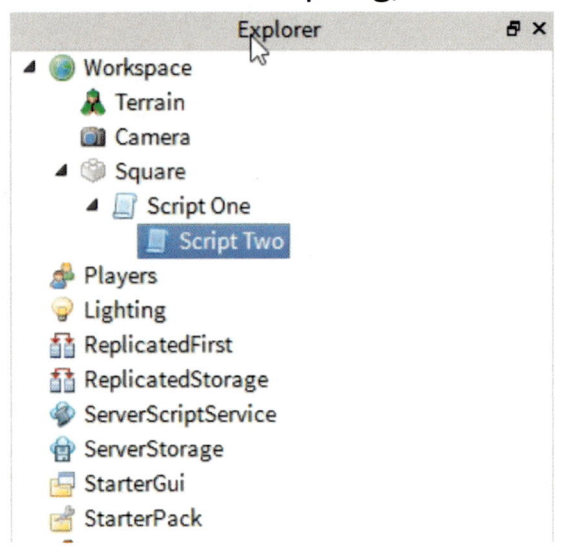

HOW TO ADD A SCRIPT OBJECT

Scripting in Lua is done inside of "Script" Objects. Scripts are usually added as Children of the Part they are working on, or as Children of Workspace if they are not working on a specific Part. To add a script:
1. Right-click the Part which will have a script inside it.
2. Go to "Insert Object".
3. Click on "Script".

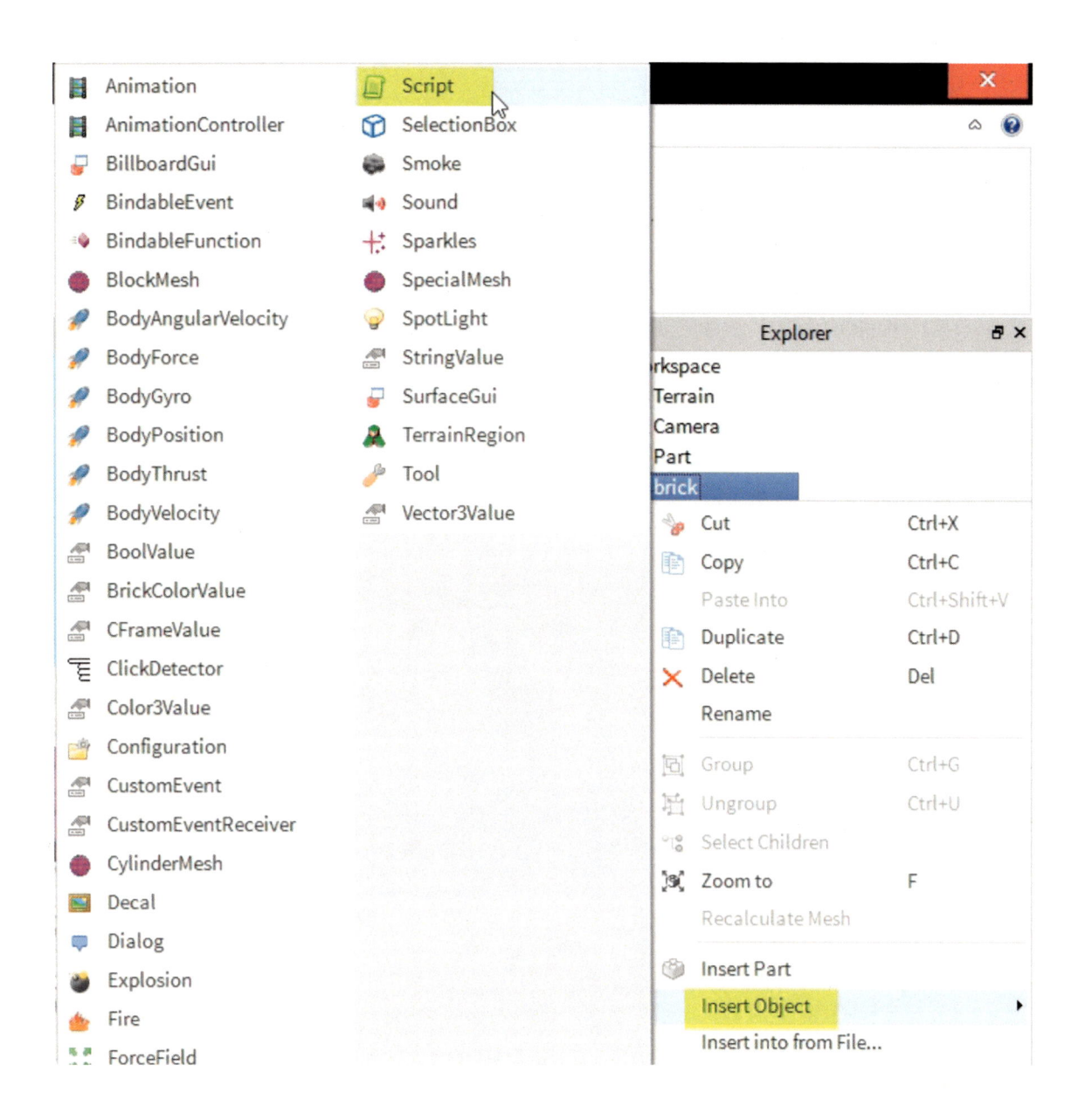

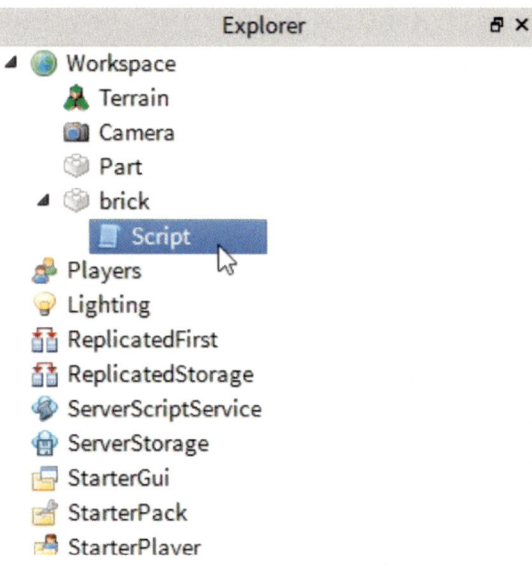

ROBLOX LUA: SCRIPTING FOR BEGINNERS

THE VERY BASICS

To look at the code inside a script object, double-click it in the Explorer. Whenever you make a new Script, it will automatically say:

```
print 'Hello World!'
```

This will just type the text "Hello World!" in the Output box when you test the game. Try changing the text inside the apostrophes to make your own text come up, for example:

```
print 'I am awesome!'
```

See it come up in the Output box when you press Play.

```
Output
14:11:31.651 - Use the new http api: no
14:15:29.369 - Auto-Saving...
I am awesome!
```

NIFTY NUGGET: Try typing a "print" line in the Command Bar. This will also print your text to the Output box.

VARIABLES

Variables are a really important part of scripting. A variable is anything that holds **information which can change**. In ROBLOX Lua, to make a variable we just type out what name we want to give our variable and what we want the variable to be equal to, for example:

```
score = 3
x = 1000
myNumber = 11
```

This is an example of a number variable, but there are other types of variables too – not just numbers. A variable that holds text is known as a "String". Here are some examples of strings:

```
name = "Joe1090"
text = "I love scripting!"
```

Notice that a string has to be written in double quotation marks, and that when you write a string, the string text will turn purple.

The other important type of variable is a Boolean. Booleans can only be "true" or "false". A Boolean is not a string, because it is not text. A Boolean is basically like yes or no, and on or off. Writing a Boolean would look like this:

```
switch = true
y = false
```

MAKING VARIABLES AS OBJECTS

When you right-click a Part and select Insert Object, there are options which allow you to create variables. These are:

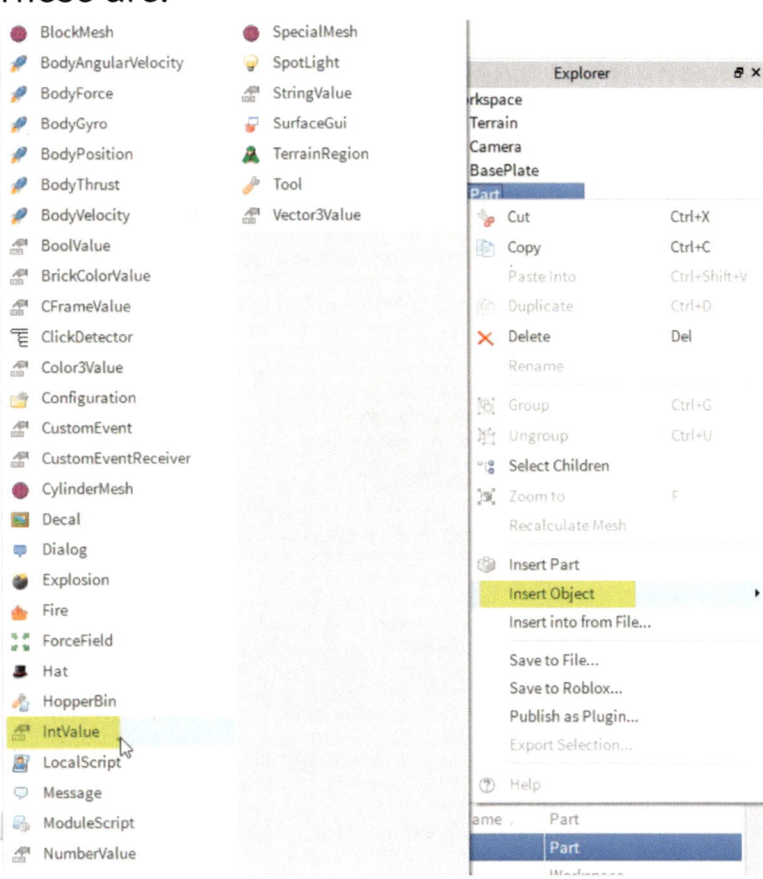

THE VERY BASICS

- IntValue – this produces a variable which is a **whole number**, for example 1, 5 or 10. Click on the IntValue in the Explorer, and then go to it's Properties. There is a property called **Value**, which I have changed to 50, and another property called Name. Making an IntValue in this way is essentially the same as writing:

```
a = 50
```

But gives you much more control because it's easy to use this variable in other scripts.

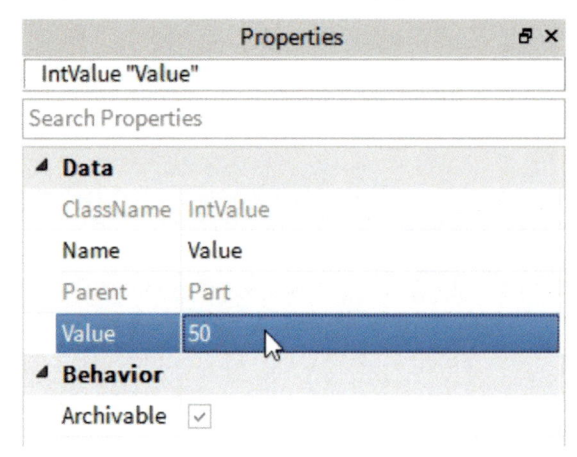

- NumberValue – this is a variable which can be **any number**, not just a whole number, for example 1.4, 5.1 or 10.313. Generally, you won't be using NumberValue much, and it's easier to stick to IntValue.
- BoolValue – this produces a Boolean, which can have a **Value** of true or false.
- StringValue – produces a string of text, which has a **Value** made from letters.

PRINTING VARIABLES

Sometimes, we will want to use print to find out the Value of a variable. If the variable is:

```
x = 54
```

Then to print it, our script would say:

```
x = 54
print(x)
```

Or if it was a string:

```
x = "ROBLOX is fun"
print(x)
```

If we had two variables, we can even use the print function to do maths for us:

```
x = 12
y = 5
print(x + y)
```

To subtract we would use print(x – y), to multiply we would use print(x * y) and to divide we would use print(x / y). Try to use the print function with variables to do the following sums:
- 5 * 20
- 30 / 10 - 2

CREATING VARIABLES WITH SCRIPT

You can also add variable Objects using script. This is going to be a great way for us to learn how to define objects, make new objects and get more comfortable with scripting. It's important that you try this out for yourself. Let's do it:
1. Insert a new script object as a Child of Workspace.
2. Double-click it to open up the script.
3. Delete the script that is already there.
4. Type the following script:

```
myVariable = Instance.new("IntValue")
```

You can write anything you want for the word "myVariable" – this is just a shortcut which you use when talking about the new Object. The Instance.new command produces a new Object. Whatever you put into the quotation marks inside the brackets, is the Object you will make - we need to write "IntValue" in the brackets because we want to make an IntValue Object (for example, if we wanted to make a BoolValue Object, we would need to type "BoolValue" into the brackets).

THE VERY BASICS

However, it's not enough to write just this, because right now the new Object is simply floating around in thin air – it needs a Parent:

    5.   Type the new script:

```
myVariable = Instance.new("IntValue")
myVariable.Parent = Workspace
```

By typing the second line, we have defined where we want our new IntValue Object to go. Try testing the script by pressing Play, then take a look inside Workspace and find the IntValue Object. When you press Stop, the IntValue Object will disappear again.

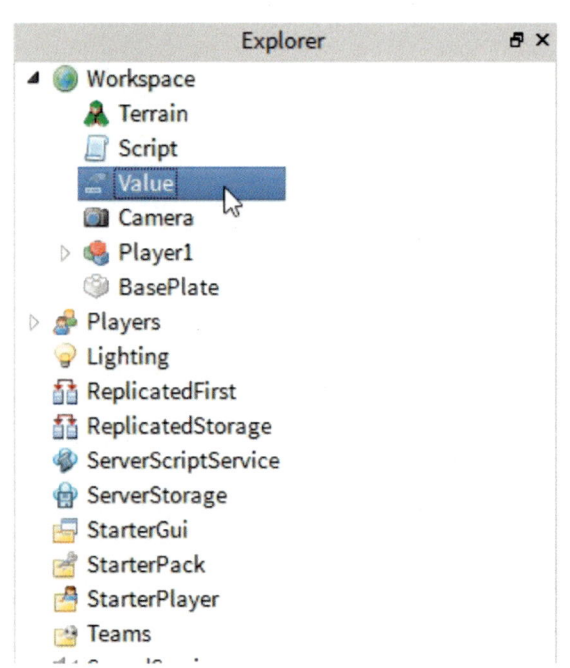

    6.   We can use this system to define other things about the new IntValue Object:

```
myVariable = Instance.new("IntValue")
myVariable.Parent = Workspace
myVariable.Name = "anyWordHere"
myVariable.Value = 10
```

Are you starting to see the pattern? You can use the shortcut you've given to the new Object (I used "myVariable"), followed by a full stop, followed by the name of a property, and then an equals sign to set that property to anything you like.

ROBLOX LUA: SCRIPTING FOR BEGINNERS

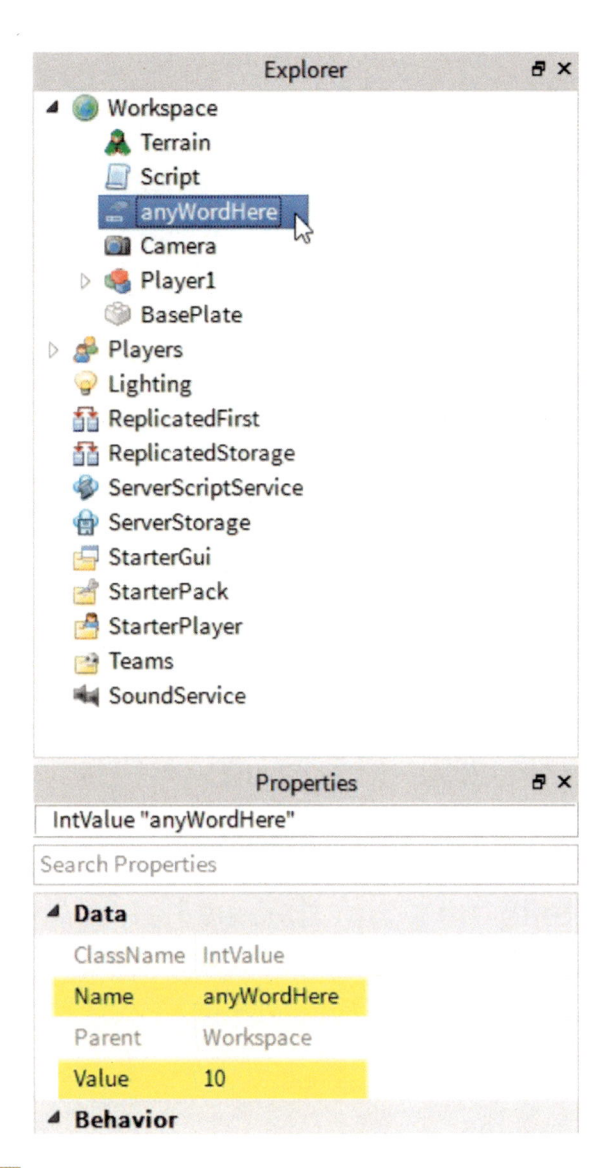

CHALLENGE

Try to make a new BoolValue Object in the Workspace when the game loads called "newBool", and which has a Value of false, using script. If you get stuck, take a look at the code above and think about:

• What will you need to write in the brackets after Instance.new to make a BoolValue Object instead of an IntValue Object?
• Are you putting full stops and spaces in the right place?

FUNCTIONS AND EVENTS
WRITING A FUNCTION

Functions are something you will be using all the time. A function is a set of instructions. An event is something which we can use to **call** the function. To **call a function** means to make it run. Writing a function is really easy:
1. Let's make a new Place.
2. Add a new script Object as a Child of Workspace.
3. To make a function, we write:

```
function cat()
end
```

Writing the word 'function' tells our script that we are beginning to write our set of instructions. We can then use any word to give our function a name – I used the word "cat", but any word will do. After our function's name, we need to write brackets "()". Don't worry about what the brackets do for now.

If you press Enter on your keyboard, the word "end" will be added automatically to the end of the function. "end" tells the script that we have finished writing our function.

4. Our instructions need to go between the function's start and "end". Let's make a simple print function:

```
function cat()
print "I love cats"
end
```

That's it – our function is done. However, if you try testing the game by pressing Play, nothing will be printed in the Output box. This is because we have made a function, but we haven't told our script when to **call the function** and make it **run**.

CALLING FUNCTIONS AND USING EVENTS

The simplest way to call a function is to just write it's name in the script, like this:

```
function cat()
print "I love cats"
end

cat()
```

Try testing this out by pressing Play. It will now say "I love cats" in the Output box. Another way to call functions is by using Events. Let's try using an Event to call our "cat" function when we step on a Part:

1. Make a new Place.
2. Insert a new Part as a Child of Workspace.
3. Insert a new script Object as a Child of the new Part.

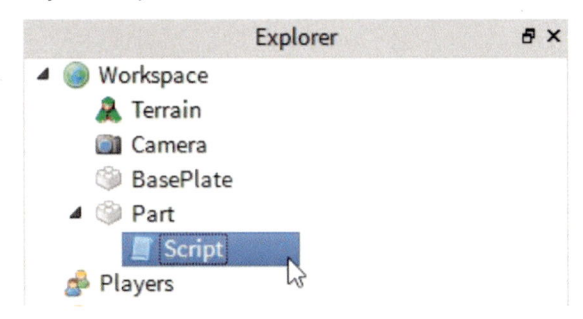

4. Write out our "cat" function:

```
function cat()
print "I love cats"
end
```

5. Now, we will add another line after this which will tell our script to write "I love cats" in the Output box whenever we touch the new brick we've added. First, we write the function:

FUNCTIONS AND EVENTS

```
function cat()
print "I love cats"
end

script.Parent.Touched
```

The last line, script.Parent.Touched is going to be the event for when we want the function to work. The brick is the script's Parent, and when it is touched, we want the function to run. But this line isn't done. To finish it up:

6. Write:

```
function cat()
print "I love cats"
end

script.Parent.Touched:connect(cat)
```

So what have we done here? After the event (script.Parent.Touched), we need to write a colon followed by the word "connect" to tell our script exactly which function it needs to run when the Part is touched. The name of the function goes in the brackets after "connect", so we need to write "cat" here.

Test the script out. When you step on the brick, "I love cats" will be written in the Output box.

NIFTY NUGGET: You can have more than one function in a script.

By now, you should understand how variables work and how to make them, how functions work and how to make a function run. We should know that variables are pieces of **information which can change**, functions are **instructions** and events **turn on the set of instructions**.

> *NIFTY NUGGET: You can see all of the different possible Events and pieces of script which you can use with a specific Object by going into Object Browser. Go to the "View" tab and click on "Object Browser". Scroll down to "Part" and click on it to open all the script which you can use with the Part Object. Scroll down the other box and you will be able to find "Touched". Lightning bolts mean that word can be used as an event – like "Touched".*

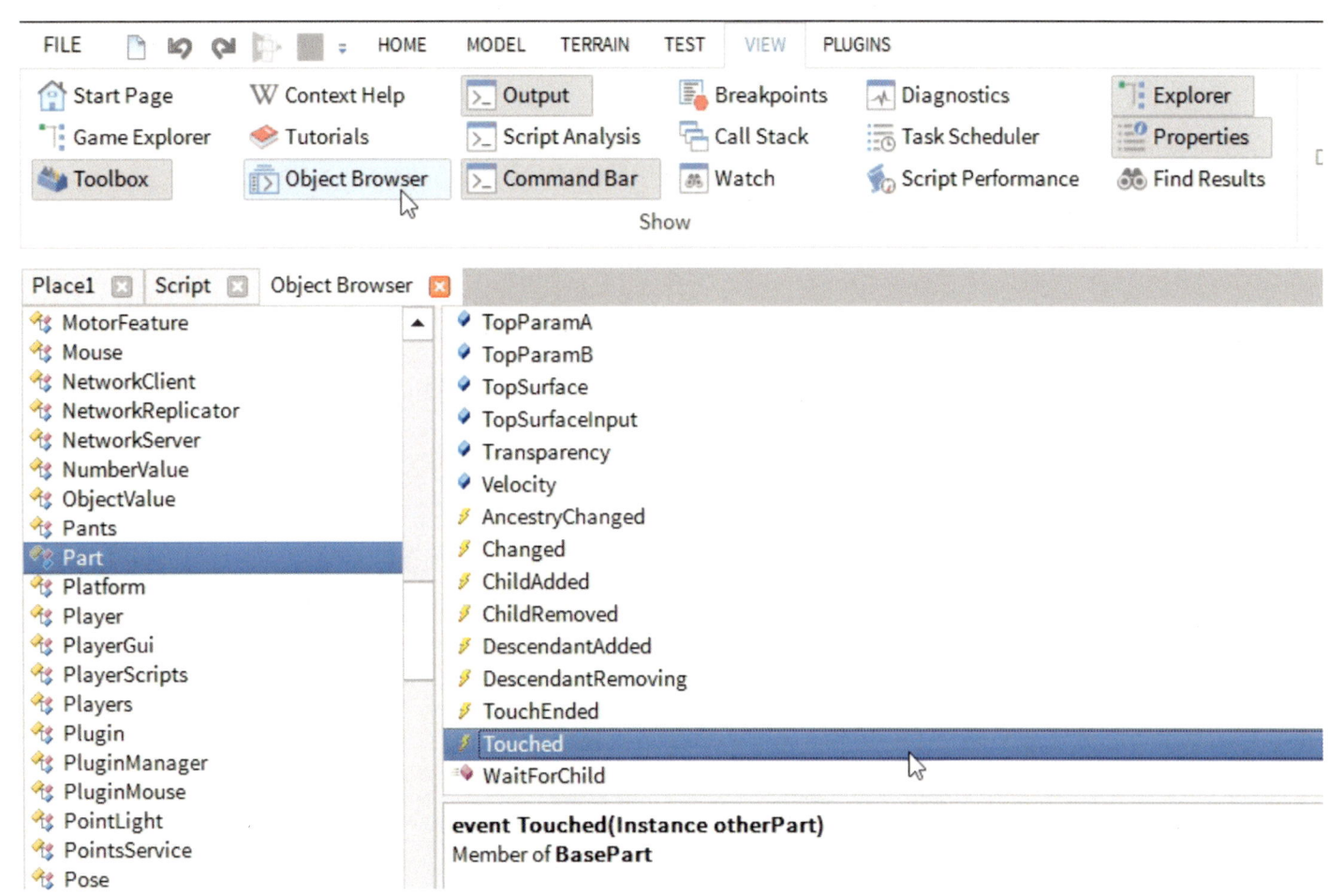

You may notice that standing on the brick causes the "I love cats" message to appear loads of times in the Output box. This is because every time the brick detects that a character is touching it, it will re-run the function, which will re-write our message.

In the next section, we will take a look at using a "debounce" to stop this from happening. This is going to be a good way to practise using variables and functions together.

FUNCTIONS AND EVENTS

USING DEBOUNCE

The easiest way to make stop an event running over and over many times when we don't want it to is by using a "debounce". For example, if you want a player to get a tool when they step on a brick, you can use debounce so the player only gets one copy of the tool instead of lots. Or, if you're making a sword, you can use debounce so that when someone is attacked by the sword, they only lose health once instead of losing health over and over in a very short time.

A debounce can be any variable, but we will use a Boolean. Remember that a Boolean is something which can **only be true or false**.

This means that we can think about using Booleans to:
- Let our function run when the Boolean is **true**.
- Stop our function from running when the Boolean is **false**.

In terms of making our debounce, this means:
- To start with, we need the Boolean to be **true** so our function can be turned on.
- When the function starts running, we need to **switch the Boolean to false** so that **the function can't be turned on again**.
- We need to make a delay of a couple of seconds, then we can **switch the Boolean to true again** so that **we can turn the function on again** when we step on our brick again.

Let's try this out:
1. We will use the same Place we just used for the last tutorial and just build on the script which we had before.
2. Our script should currently say:

```
function cat()
print "I love cats"
end

script.Parent.Touched:connect(cat)
```

3. So now let's add our new Boolean:

```
myBoolean = true

function cat()
print "I love cats"
end

script.Parent.Touched:connect(cat)
```

4. Now, we need our function to only run if myBoolean = true, and to stop running if myBoolean = false:

```
myBoolean = true

function cat()
if myBoolean == false then return end
print "I love cats"
end

script.Parent.Touched:connect(cat)
```

The "if" line means that if our Boolean is false, then the "return" phrase can be used to tell the function to stop. Using "if" and "then" with a variable in-between means that:
- **if** myBoolean is equal to **false: then** stop the function.
- **if** myBoolean is equal to **true then** this line is skipped and we go to the next one.

NIFTY NUGGET: We use a double equals sign to mean "is equal to". One equals sign means "change to".

FUNCTIONS AND EVENTS

5. Next, we need to set myBoolean to **false** when the function starts, add a delay then set myBoolean to **true** again before it finishes so that the function can be re-run. This will mean that while the function is running, it can't be re-activated because myBoolean is **false** and as we saw above, when myBoolean is false the function is stopped:

```
myBoolean = true

function cat()
if myBoolean == false then return end
myBoolean = false
print "I love cats"
wait(2)
myBoolean = true
end

script.Parent.Touched:connect(cat)
```

To add the delay, we just need to write "wait" followed by a number in brackets. The number is how many seconds we want the script to wait for.

Test this script out by pressing Play. As you can see, you can only print the text to the output box by stepping on the brick once every two seconds. Try changing the number in the brackets to change the length of the delay.

ANOTHER WAY TO WRITE FUNCTIONS

We can also write functions in the same line as an event, by just writing our function into the brackets after "connect". The above script would look like this:

```
myBoolean = true

script.Parent.Touched:connect(function()
if myBoolean == false then return end
myBoolean = false
print "I love cats"
wait(2)
myBoolean = true
end)
```

Test this out. It will work exactly the same as the previous script. However, when we write a function this way, we don't give the function a name – it doesn't need one, because we are already telling our script when to call the function. The script will call the function when it's Parent (so the brick) is touched. So we just write out the function inside the brackets after "connect". That's why we need to write a bracket after end: to close the brackets after "connect" up.

Usually, we would use the normal way that we've practised earlier to make functions. However, this way can also be useful, and we will take a look at it in a later tutorial.

CHALLENGE

The next challenge is to script a brick that changes it's BrickColor to a random color when you step on it. The script should include a debounce. Try doing this one from scratch and making a new Place – use the guide if you get stuck. There are some things you need to bear in mind:
- BrickColor is a property – this means that to change it we will need to write:

```
script.Parent.BrickColor
```

- To change the BrickColor, you need to use an equals sign, the property and then a full stop followed by Random(). It should look like this:

```
script.Parent.BrickColor = BrickColor.Random()
```

Are you getting stuck? Think about the following:
- Where do you need to put this line in the script?
- Have you got your Boolean lines in the right places?

MORE ON SCRIPTING
SCRIPT OBJECT'S LOCATION

When we are using a script Object, sometimes it doesn't actually matter where we put it. That's because we can tell a script where to put an Object, or which Object it needs to change using the Parent and Child system. This is easy, let's try it out:

1. Make a new Place and add a Script and a Part as children of Workspace.

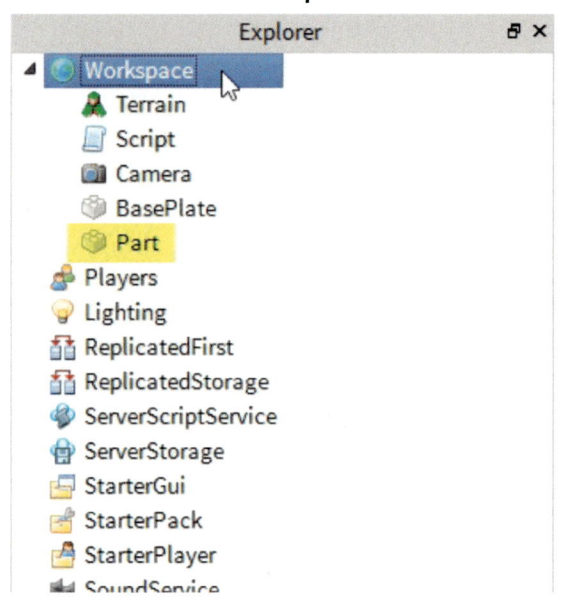

2. Now, we want our script to code for the Part we've just added. But Script isn't a child of Part! That's not a problem. This time, we'll be making a script which makes copies of (clones) the Part when we step on it:

```
function cloneBrick()
game.Workspace.Part:clone().Parent = Workspace
end

game.Workspace.Part.Touched:connect(cloneBrick)
```

As you may have noticed, the way we tell our script to clone a Part is different from what we've done before. If you take a look at the Object Browser, scroll down to Part and look at "clone()", it'll tell you what the clone() function does in the bottom box, and you may notice that clone has a purple box icon next to it (not a lightning bolt icon like Touched has).

ROBLOX LUA: SCRIPTING FOR BEGINNERS

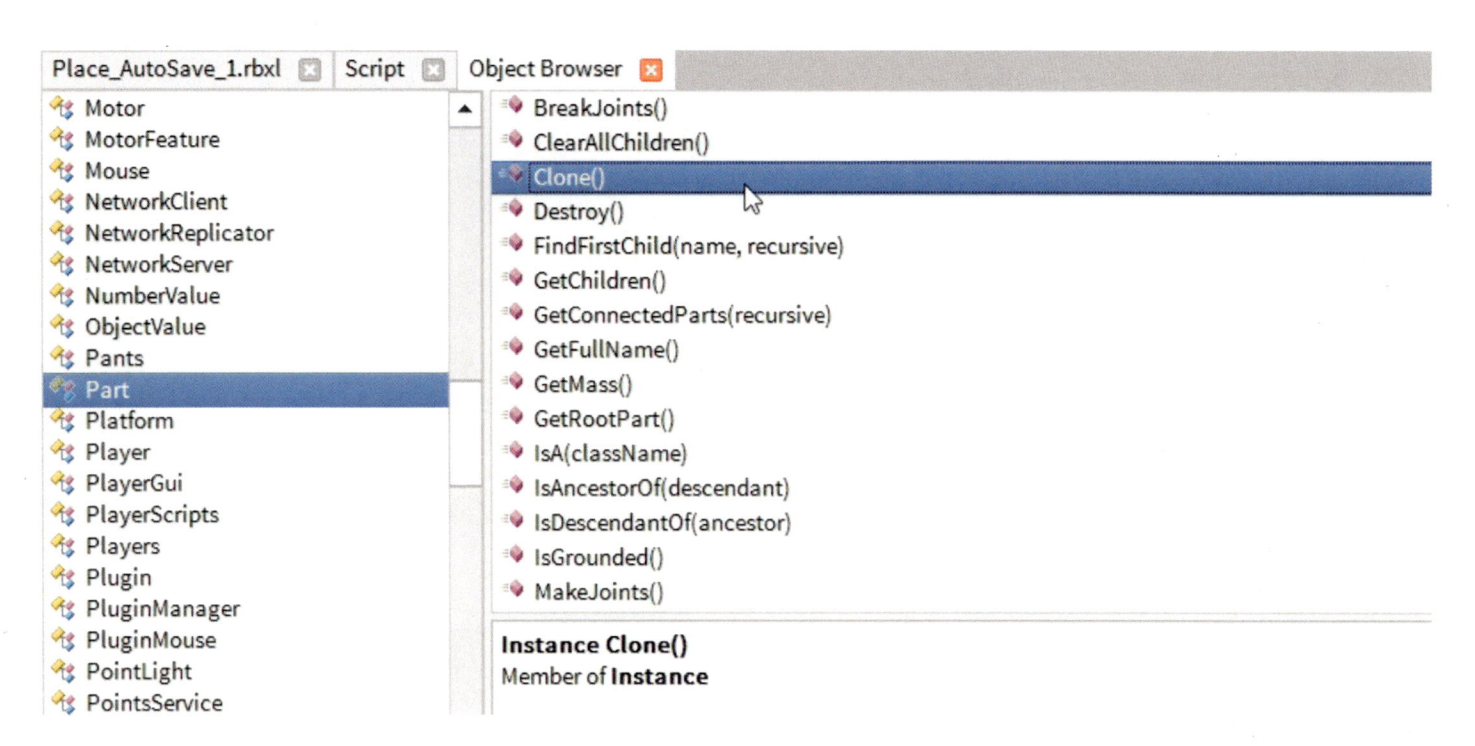

Things with a purple box icon are scripted in the above way because they have a different way of working to Events. These work on Instances. This means that we need to define what we are changing first (in this case, it's game.Workspace.Part) then a colon, then the word "clone()". Then, we need to define the new Part's Parent, to tell the new Parts where to go.

To tell our script which Part it's going to make copies of, we need to write game.Workspace.Part. The ".Part" bit is just the name of the Part. You can change the Name property of the Part and this will still work. Let's change the Part's name to "apple" and try it again:

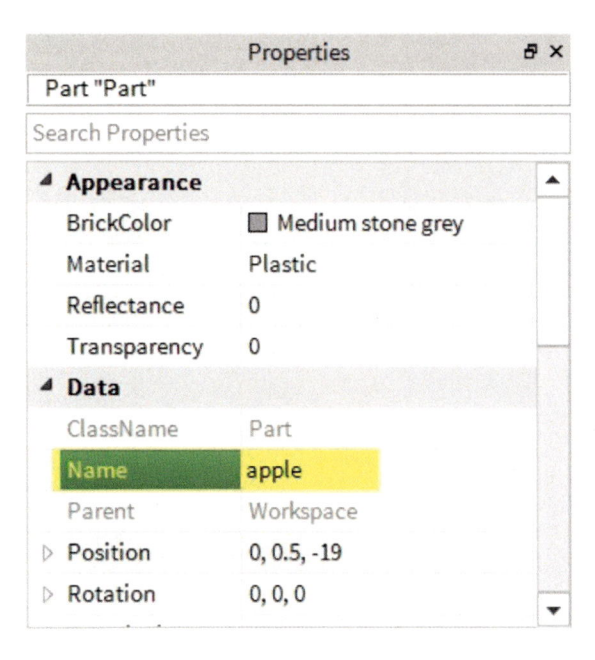

MORE ON SCRIPTING

```
function cloneBrick()
game.Workspace.apple:clone().Parent = Workspace
end

game.Workspace.apple.Touched:connect(cloneBrick)
```

3.   If you try testing the script, you'll notice that stepping on the Part causes the script to go absolutely crazy and produces millions of new Parts, and the game gets laggy really quickly. To stop this we can just add a debounce. We've covered debounces before and you should be familiar with it. Try adding a debounce to this script by yourself. If you get stuck, I've done it here so you can take a look:

```
bool = true

function cloneBrick()
if bool == false then return end
bool = false
game.Workspace.apple:clone().Parent = Workspace
wait(1)
bool = true
end

game.Workspace.apple.Touched:connect(cloneBrick)
```

SHORTCUTS IN SCRIPTS

We can use a shortcut for "game.Workspace.apple" so we don't have to type it all out every time. We just add a line of code at the top, and then every time we would have written the full "game.Workspace.apple" out, we just write the shortcut word instead. This can be anything. I'll use "ping" just to demonstrate it:

```
bool = true
ping = game.Workspace.apple

function cloneBrick()
if bool == false then return end
bool = false
ping:clone().Parent = Workspace
wait(1)
bool = true
end

ping.Touched:connect(cloneBrick)
```

Test this out, it will work just as well as the full "game.Workspace.apple" but it's easier and quicker to write.

GUIs
WHAT IS A GUI?

GUI stands for "Graphical User Interface". This picture shows an example of a GUI.

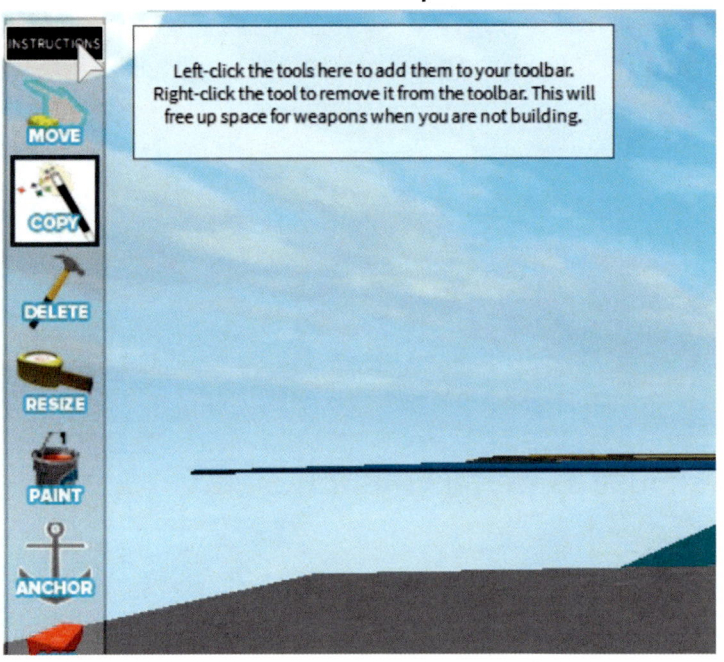

GUIs are used to show information, pictures or to hold buttons. We can use script to make these buttons do things when they are clicked.

GUIs can be on a player's screen (in which case they are a ScreenGUI), on one of the surfaces of a Part (these are SurfaceGUIs), and another type which is on a Part but will always face the player – these are called BillboardGUIs.

ScreenGUIs are put into the StarterGUI folder in the Explorer. SurfaceGUI and BillboardGUI need to be children of a Part.

ROBLOX LUA: SCRIPTING FOR BEGINNERS

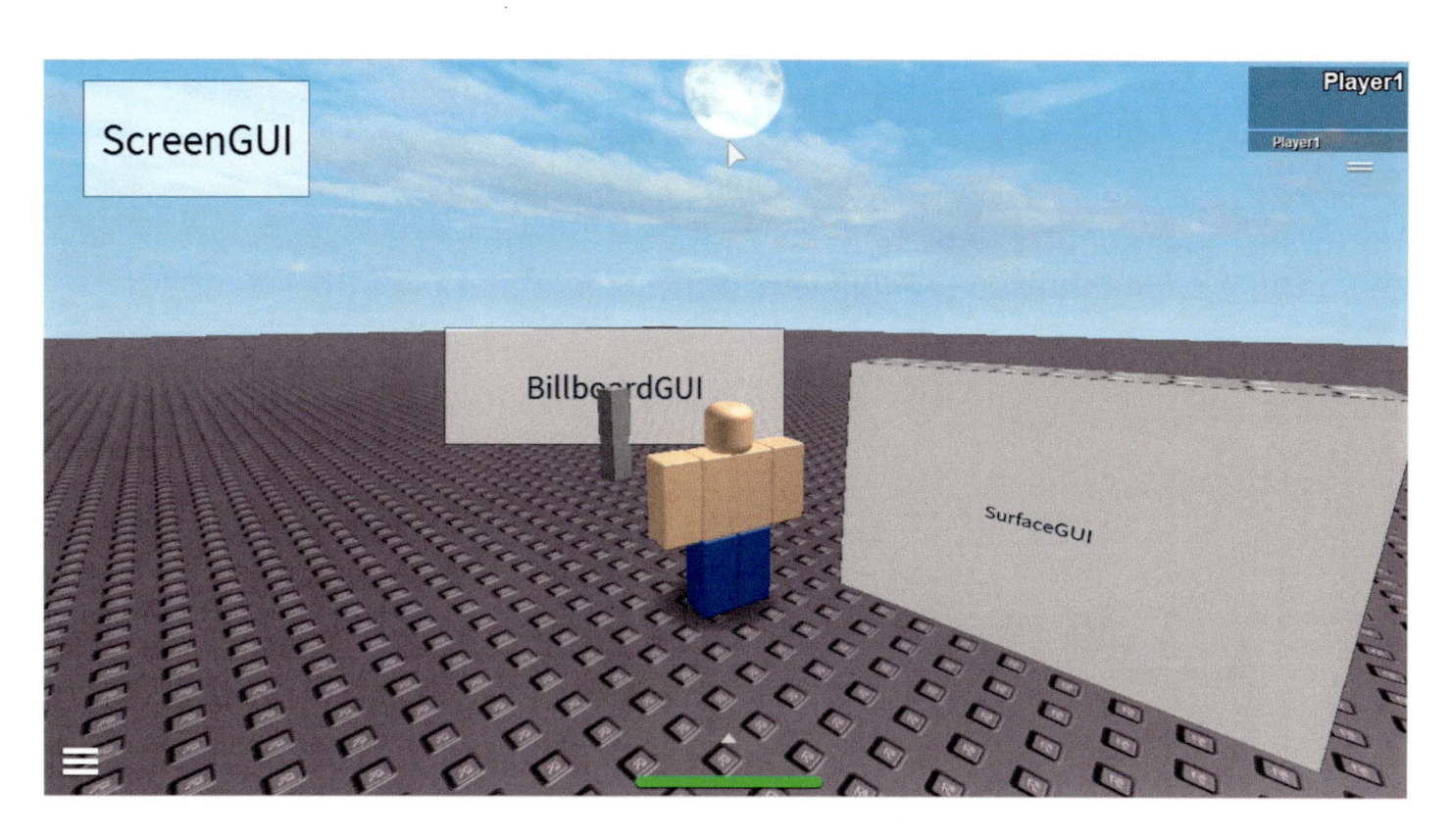

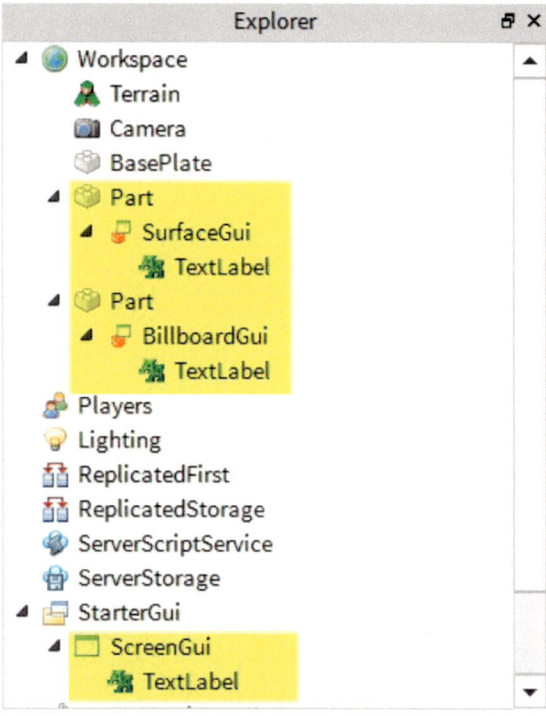

GUIs and their location in the Explorer

GUIs

OBJECTS WE CAN PUT INSIDE GUIs

There are 5 main Objects that we use a GUI to display. I'll show you this using a ScreenGUI. To add a ScreenGUI, right-click the StarterGUI folder in the Explorer and select ScreenGUI. We can then add the following Objects as children of the ScreenGUI:

TEXTLABEL

A TextLabel is just a box with a border, background and text inside. This is mainly used for titles, labels and giving the player information.

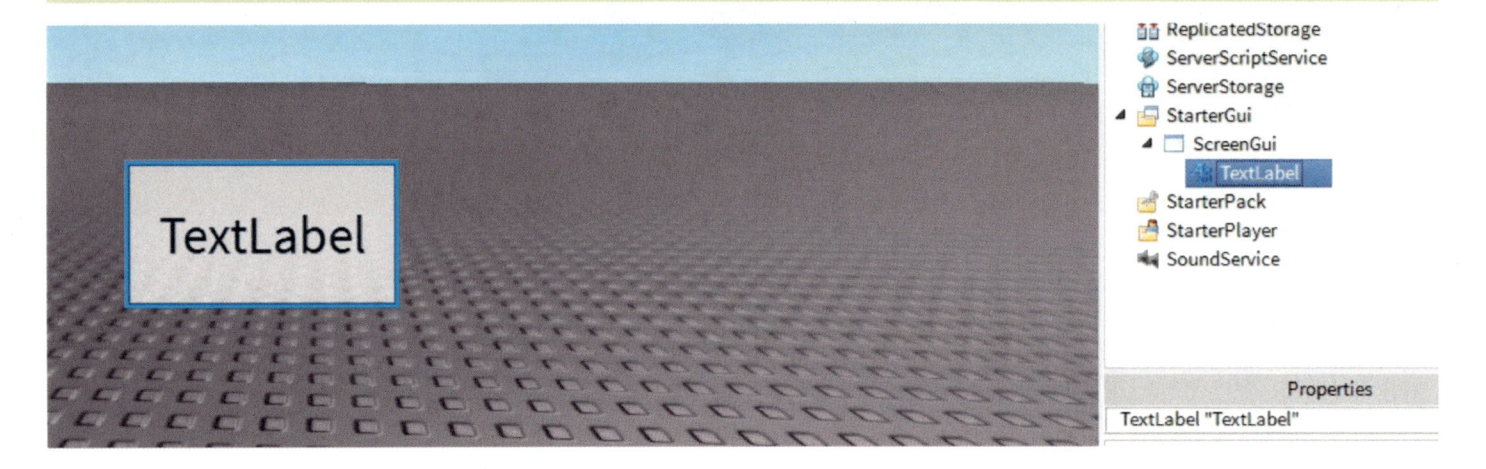

TEXTBOX

A TextBox is also a box with a border, background and text. However, if the player clicks on the TextBox they can type their own text.

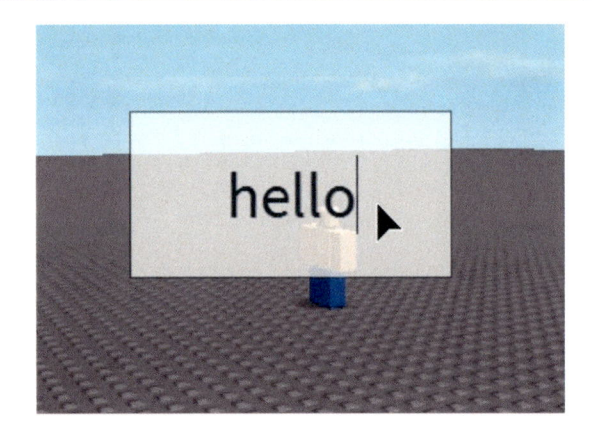

TEXTBUTTON

TextButtons look the same as TextLabels and TextBoxes, but you can add a script which lets them run functions when they're clicked by the player.

If you add a TextButton and try testing the game, you will see that the color of the TextButton changes when you mouse over it. This is a good sign to people that are playing your game that this is a button which can be clicked.

IMAGELABEL

ImageLabels are used to add pictures to GUIs. To add your own image, you need to first add the picture you want to your game as a Decal. Then, go to the Decal's Texture property. Copy this text, and paste it into the Image property of the ImageLabel.

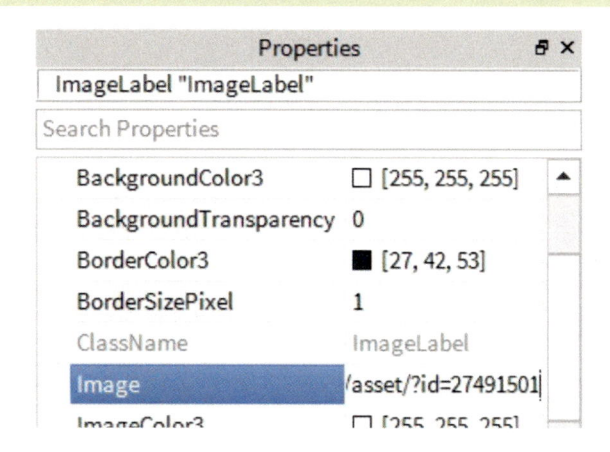

GUIs

45

IMAGEBUTTON

Again, ImageButtons are basically ImageLabels which have more events possible for you to script with. Like TextButtons, they can run functions when clicked.

PROPERTIES OF GUI OBJECTS

Here are the most important properties of both Text and Image Objects:

BACKGROUNDCOLOR3

This is the color of the box which the text or image is inside of. Try changing the color of the background using this property.

BACKGROUNDTRANSPARENCY

The higher the transparency is (from 0 to 1), the more see-through the background will be.

BORDERCOLOR3

This is the color of the line around the background.

BORDERSIZEPIXEL

This changes the thickness of the line around the background.

POSITION

This is the place on the screen where the GUI Object is located. The way we use the position property is new to you – here's how it works. The first set of {0, 0} brackets is for the x-position. The x-position is how far right it is. The second set of {0, 0} brackets is for the y-position. This is how far down the screen the GUI Object is.

The first number in the {0, 0} brackets is for how far along the player's screen the position will be, on a scale from 0 to 1. So if the x-position is {0, 0}, the GUI Object will be on the very left of the player's screen. If the x-position is {1, 0}, the GUI Object will be on the far right of the player's screen.

The second number in the {0, 0} brackets is called the Offset – this is how many extra pixels we want to shift our GUI Object. So if we put {0, 20} for the y-position, the GUI Object will be shifted down 20 pixels from the top of the screen.

SIZE

The brackets here work in the same way as they did for Position. This property changes how big the GUI Object is on the screen.

GUIs

To be able to change the text in Text Objects, you will need to be familiar with their Text properties:

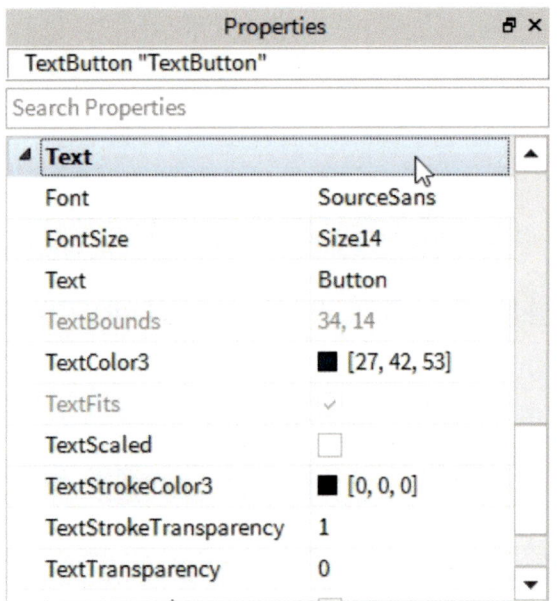

FONT AND FONTSIZE

Font will change what style of the letters, and FontSize will change the size of the letters.

TEXT

Whatever you type here will be what shows up on the player's screen inside the Text Object.

TEXTCOLOR3 AND TEXTSTROKECOLOR3

TextColor3 changes the color of the text, while TextStrokeColor3 changes the color of the border around the text.

TEXT/TEXTSROKETRANSPARENCY

These change how see-through the text and the text's outline is. TextStrokeTransparency is normally set to 1, so you need to decrease it to be able to see the text's outline.

TEXTXALIGNMENT AND TEXTYALIGNMENT

These change the position of the text inside the Text Object. Try them out and see where each option puts your text.

NIFTY NUGGET: If you are making a toolbar or window that will contain other GUI Objects, you can create a Frame as a child of ScreenGUI, and then add the GUI Objects as children of the Frame. Using a Frame means that the first number in the {0, 0} brackets will scale the Size and Position of GUI Objects to the size of the Frame – so if you did {1,0}, {1,0} for Position, the GUI Object would be in the bottom-right corner of the Frame and not the screen.

SCRIPTING OUR GUI

Okay, so we know how to make GUIs and GUI Objects. Now, let's learn how to use a TextButton to make new Parts appear:
1. Make a new Place.
2. Create a ScreenGUI as a child of StarterGUI, and a TextButton as a child of ScreenGUI. Then, add a Script Object as a child of TextButton.

GUIs

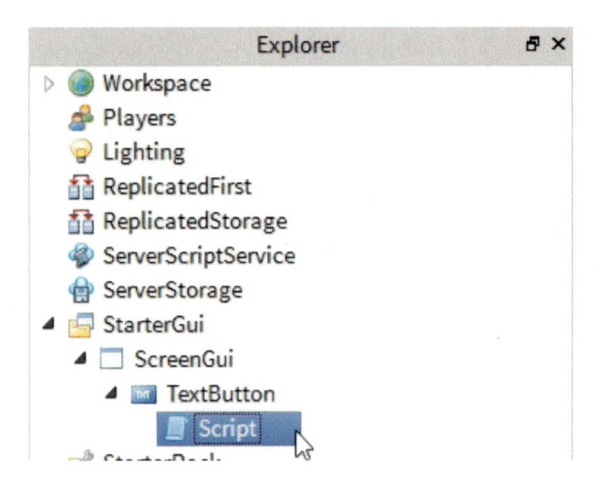

3. Practise changing some of the properties of your button to make it look however you want it to.

4. Let's type out our function for making a new Part:

```
function newBrick()
brick = Instance.new("Part")
brick.Parent = Workspace
brick.Position = Vector3.new(0, 0, 0)
brick.Size = Vector3.new(2, 2, 2)
end
```

We haven't practised setting Size or Position with script before. Because size and position have 3 dimensions (they have an x-axis or length, y-axis or height, and z-axis or width) we need to use the term "Vector3" – we use Vector3 whenever we are changing a property that has 3 dimensions. We write Vector3, followed by new because we are setting a new Vector3 value, followed by the (x, y, z) numbers we want.

5. Now, we need to add an event line to connect our function

```
function newBrick()
brick = Instance.new("Part")
brick.Parent = Workspace
brick.Position = Vector3.new(0, 0, 0)
brick.Size = Vector3.new(2, 2, 2)
end

script.Parent.MouseButton1Click:connect(newBrick)
```

We can use "MouseButton1Click" as an event when we have a TextButton or an ImageButton. This means the function will be activated when we click on the TextButton with the left mouse button.

NIFTY NUGGET: There are loads of events which can be used with a TextButton, for example "MouseEnter" which runs the function once when you move your mouse over the TextButton. Try checking them out in the Object Browser, under "TextButton".

LEADERBOARD
SCRIPT-THROUGH #1
INTRODUCTION TO SCRIPT-THROUGH

In the next few chapters of this book, I will write up a script step by step so that you can learn new things while also being able to see the rules you've already learned being applied. These chapters are not just examples, you will also learn new ideas important to scripting here, so don't skip them.

In the first script-through, I'll teach you how to make a Leaderboard with Points and Deaths on it. We will make coins which give us Points and then disappear when we walk into them, and we will take a look at the way Players, Characters and Humanoids work in ROBLOX Lua.

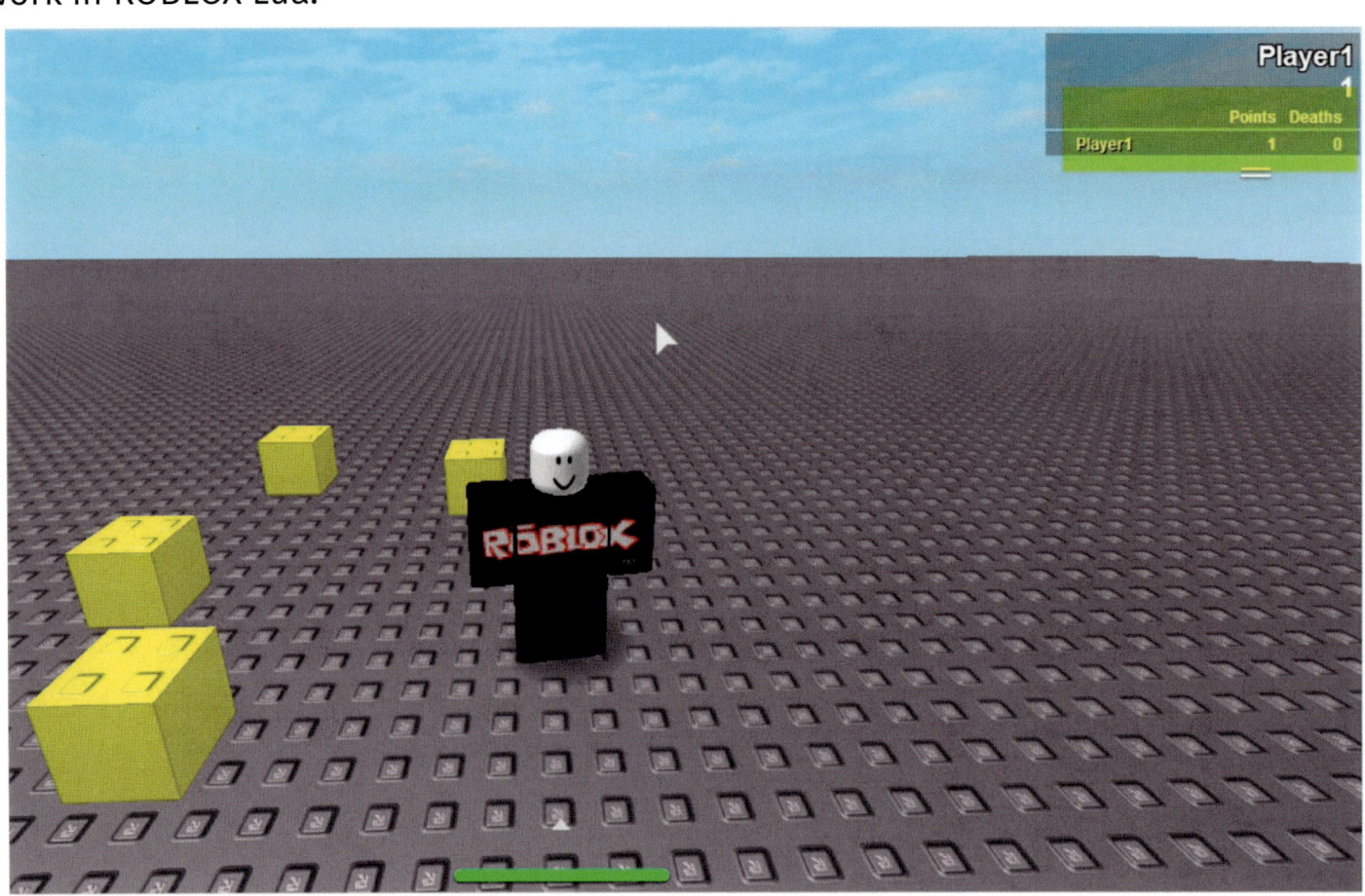

CREATING THE LEADERBOARD

Add a Script as a child of Workspace. This is where we will our leaderboard script will go.

A leaderboard is an IntValue Object that's a child of the player. The different columns we want to add to our leaderboard (we will be using Points and Deaths) then need to be added as children of the leaderboard. To begin with, we need a function to tell our script when to add a player's leaderboard:

```
game.Players.PlayerAdded:connect(function(player)
end)
```

This is that alternative way of making functions which we saw in the Functions and Events chapter. The event is "PlayerAdded", and since we wrote game.Players.PlayerAdded, this function will run whenever a new player is added to the Players folder in the Explorer. (This happens every time a new player joins the game).

We also need to write "player" in the brackets after function – something that is written into the brackets after the word "function" is called a "parameter". The parameter "player" can be used with the event "PlayerAdded" – what does it do? Typing "player" into these brackets means that **this function only runs for the player who was just added**. So only the new player will have a leaderboard added. If we didn't write this, every player would be given another leaderboard each time a new player joined the game and the script would break.

Now, let's add a new Instance of our Leaderboard:

```
game.Players.PlayerAdded:connect(function(player)
stats = Instance.new("IntValue")
stats.Parent = player
stats.Name = "leaderstats"
end)
```

In order to create a leaderboard, we need our new IntValue to be called "leaderstats". Any other name, and it won't produce a leaderboard. Try testing the game now and taking a look inside "Player".

LEADERBOARD SCRIPT-THROUGH

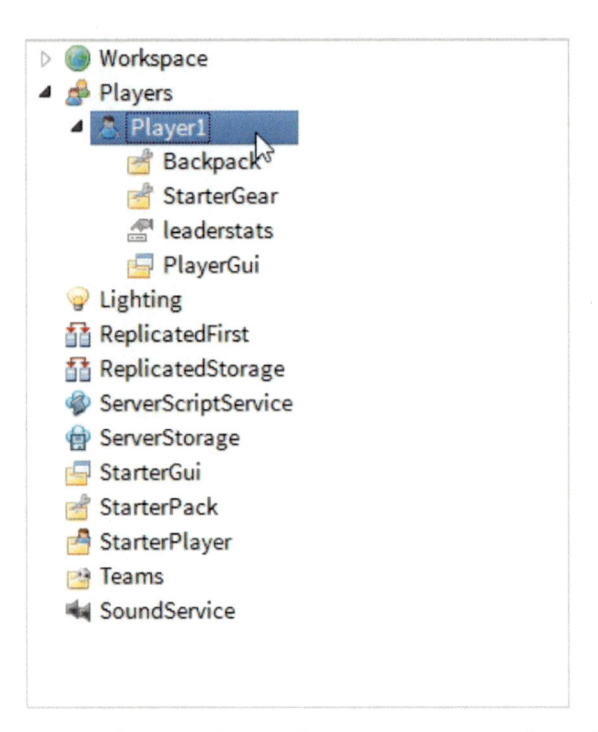

Let's start adding the Points and Deaths columns to our leaderboard:

```
game.Players.PlayerAdded:connect(function(player)
stats = Instance.new("IntValue")
stats.Parent = player
stats.Name = "leaderstats"

points = Instance.new("IntValue")
points.Parent = stats
points.Name = "Points"

deaths = Instance.new("IntValue")
deaths.Parent = stats
deaths.Name = "Deaths"
end)
```

As you can see, we need to add our columns (Deaths and Points) as children of the "leaderstats" Object. Whatever the Name properties of the Deaths and Points IntValues are will be the words that show up in the column. Try testing this script out. It should look like this.

ROBLOX LUA: SCRIPTING FOR BEGINNERS

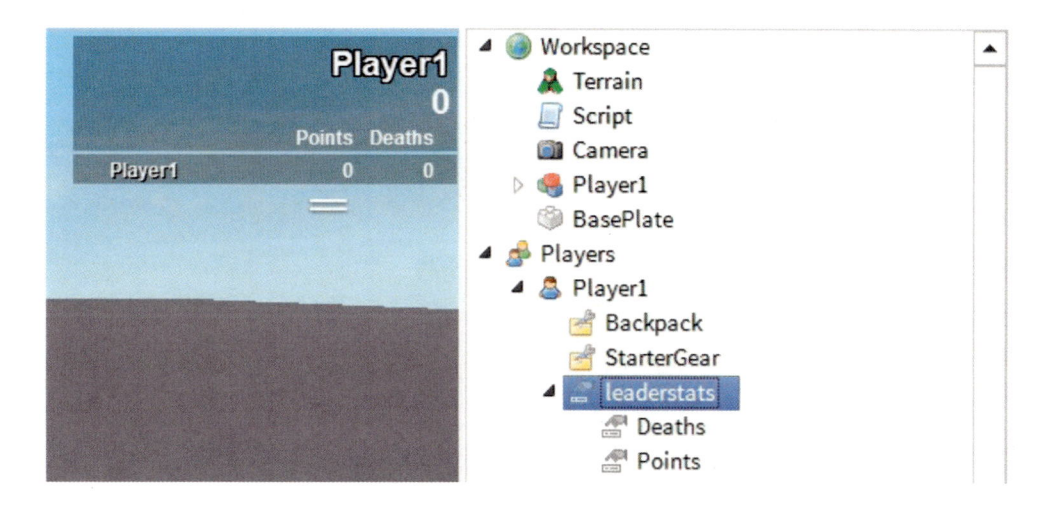

SCRIPTING A COIN THAT GIVES POINTS

So we've made a leaderboard now, but it doesn't actually do anything yet. It's just there. Let's make a script that gives us points and makes a brick disappear when we step on it. First, add a new Part and a Script as it's child. Color the Part yellow so it looks more like a coin.

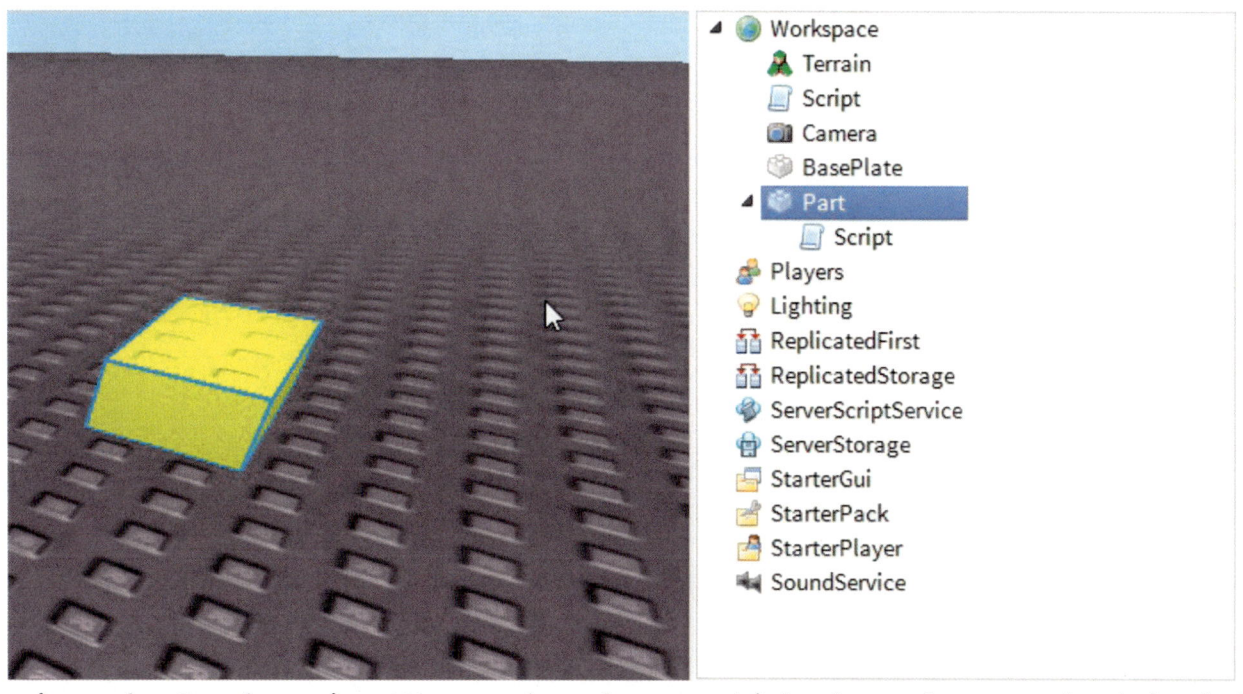

Now go into the Part's script. We need to detect which player has touched the brick, so we will start with our event line and write the function inside it:

```
script.Parent.Touched:connect(function()
end)
```

LEADERBOARD SCRIPT-THROUGH

Now, our next line will be to find which player touched the brick:

```
script.Parent.Touched:connect(function()
player = game:GetService("Players").LocalPlayer
end)
```

To find the player we need to use the "GetService" function. A "Service" is just a folder in the Explorer like Workspace, Players, Teams or StarterGUI, so by typing "GetService" then "Players" in brackets, we're telling our script to go into the Players folder.

"LocalPlayer" is used to find the player whose computer the game is running on – so if you are playing the game, you would be the LocalPlayer. If your friend was playing the game and he stepped on the brick, he would the LocalPlayer in this script. That means that our script now knows who has stepped on the brick.

Next, let's add some script to find our LocalPlayer's Points stat:

```
script.Parent.Touched:connect(function()
player = game:GetService("Players").LocalPlayer
stats = player:findFirstChild("leaderstats")
points = stats:findFirstChild("Points")
end)
```

We can locate the leaderstats Object by using the findFirstChild function because leaderstats is a child of player. We can then find Points as a child of leaderstats using the findFirstChild function, too. Now, let's give our player some points for stepping on the brick:

```
script.Parent.Touched:connect(function()
player = game:GetService("Players").LocalPlayer
stats = player:findFirstChild("leaderstats")
points = stats:findFirstChild("Points")
points.Value = points.Value + 1
end)
```

ROBLOX LUA: SCRIPTING FOR BEGINNERS

To give the player points, we need to increase the Value of their points IntValue Object. Remember that one equals sign means "change to". Our new line therefore tells the script to change the Value of Points to whatever it was before add one. The final line we need to add is to make the brick disappear after we step on it:

```
script.Parent.Touched:connect(function()
player = game:GetService("Players").LocalPlayer
stats = player:findFirstChild("leaderstats")
points = stats:findFirstChild("Points")
points.Value = points.Value + 1
script.Parent:Destroy()
end)
```

Destroy is used to remove an Object from the Workspace. Test the script out. Try adding some more coins – either duplicate them in the Explorer or script them yourself as practise.

PLAYERS, CHARACTERS, HUMANOIDS

Someone who is playing your game is a **player** - but the **player** cannot actually die. Only that player's **Humanoid** can die. A Humanoid is an object which controls that player's health, movement and detects when the player dies. Every player also has their own individual **Character** which has their own clothing, hair etc. saved – the Character is the actual bricks and decals that make up your player. When you run the game, you can see the see the Character in the Workspace.

- Player = person playing the game.
- Character = the bricks and decals a player is made up from.
- Humanoid = an object that handles the deaths, movement, jumping, sitting and health systems of a player, and many more.

> **NIFTY NUGGET:** The "Character" **property** of Player is not actually the player's Character itself because the Character is a model (a model is a group of bricks). "Player.Character" is used to point ROBLOX to that individual player's own model. You can find this model by clicking on Workspace while the game is running; it will be called "Player1".

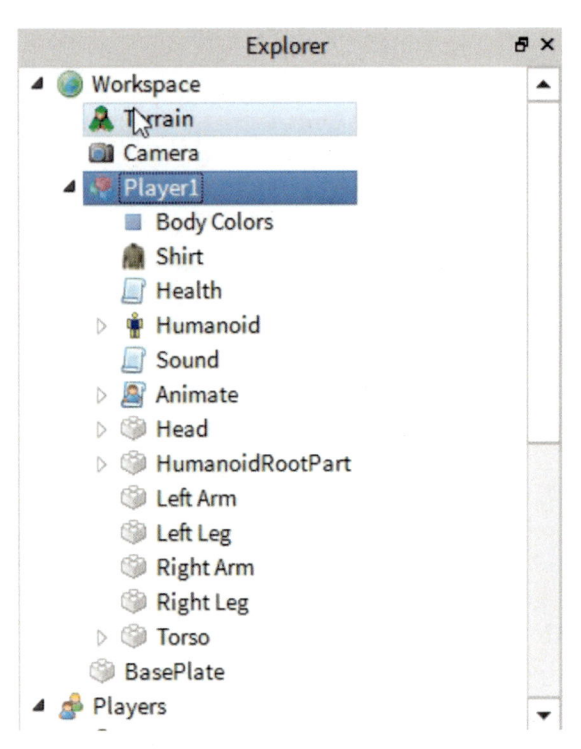

LEADERBOARD SCRIPT-THROUGH

All the parts that make up a player's Character can be found in the Workspace while the game is running.

INCREASING DEATHS WHEN A PLAYER DIES

We need to use a script which finds out when our player's Humanoid has died in order to increase that player's Deaths on the leaderboard. Let's add this into the main leaderboard script we made earlier:

```
game.Players.PlayerAdded:connect(function(player)
stats = Instance.new("IntValue")
stats.Parent = player
stats.Name = "leaderstats"

points = Instance.new("IntValue")
points.Parent = stats
points.Name = "Points"

deaths = Instance.new("IntValue")
deaths.Parent = stats
deaths.Name = "Deaths"

player.CharacterAdded:connect(function(character)
end)
end)
```

Does this look familiar? We write this **inside** our leaderboard script so that we know who "player" is and so that when *that player's* Humanoid dies, only *that player's* Deaths increase. This time, we're using the CharacterAdded function so that the next line only starts working when the player's Character has been loaded (since the game often lags on start-up, we want to wait until everything is loaded up).

NIFTY NUGGET: Every time a player dies, they are given a new Character, so using the CharacterAdded function means our script won't stop working after one death.

Now let's add a couple of lines to detect when our player's Humanoid dies and increase their Deaths value:

LEADERBOARD SCRIPT-THROUGH

```
game.Players.PlayerAdded:connect(function(player)
stats = Instance.new("IntValue")
stats.Parent = player
stats.Name = "leaderstats"

points = Instance.new("IntValue")
points.Parent = stats
points.Name = "Points"

deaths = Instance.new("IntValue")
deaths.Parent = stats
deaths.Name = "Deaths"

player.CharacterAdded:connect(function(character)
character.Humanoid.Died:connect(function()
deaths.Value = deaths.Value + 1
end)
end)
end)
```

Test out the script now. That's it for this script-through. It's quite a lot to take in – a great way to practise is to try and do it again by yourself without looking at this book, and just check back if you get stuck. Try it out!

GUI TELEPORTER
SCRIPT-THROUGH #2
INTRODUCTION TO SCRIPT-THROUGH

In this script-through, we'll be making a ScreenGUI with two buttons. We will be able to click either of these buttons to teleport our player's Humanoid to two different places. This is something that will be really useful in making your own games, for example in designing VIP areas or different worlds which players can be teleported to with the click of a button.

Make a new game and add another big piece of land which you will be able to teleport to. As well as the BasePlate, I've added a large brick in the sky which will be where clicking the button will teleport my player.

NIFTY NUGGET: Don't forget to Anchor the other brick, or it will fall down as soon as you test the game!

GUI TELEPORTER SCRIPT-THROUGH

MAKING OUR GUI

1. Add a ScreenGUI Object as a child of StarterGUI.
2. Add two TextButtons, one for the sky and one for the BasePlate. Play around with their properties to make them look nicer. When you first make them, they will both be in the same place and you will need to use the Position property to move them apart.
3. Now, you need to add LocalScripts as children of the TextButtons. A LocalScript is a like a normal Script, but it only runs on the player's computer and nobody else's. That means that we can use a LocalScript to find out which player clicked and therefore which player to teleport really easily.

Try testing the game. If you click on Players and then Player1, you will be able to find the whole of the StarterGUI folder has been copied into the player. Because we've used a LocalScript, we can just use the LocalPlayer property to find which player is pressing the button - we wouldn't be able to do that in a normal script.

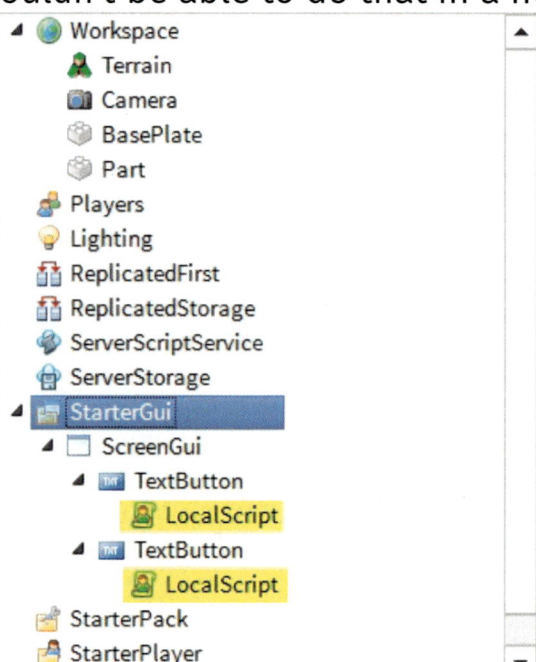

SCRIPTING THE TELEPORT

So let's script our teleporter. First, we will define our player:

```
player = game.Players.LocalPlayer
```

Next, we need to write out our function for teleporting the player:

```
player = game.Players.LocalPlayer

function Teleport()
playersCharacter = player.Character
end
```

We looked at Characters and Humanoids in the previous tutorial. In order to teleport the player, we need to teleport their Character, which is the bricks that the player is made up from.

To move a player's Character, we typically move their Torso (the middle section of the player's Character). We want to teleport them to the sky, so we need to teleport the torso to whatever the y-position of the sky brick is plus 3. Let's try finishing up the function by using the Position property:

```
player = game.Players.LocalPlayer

function Teleport()
playersCharacter = player.Character
playersCharacter.Torso.Position = Vector3.new(0, 203, 0)
end

script.Parent.MouseButton1Down:connect(Teleport)
```

Try testing the script. Uh oh! It's not working – our player seems to go invisible and leave their body behind when they teleport. That's because we're moving only the Torso and not the rest of the body. To move an entire Model with all of the Parts that are welded to it, we need to use CFrame instead of Position. CFrame works pretty much the same way:

GUI TELEPORTER SCRIPT-THROUGH

```
player = game.Players.LocalPlayer

function Teleport()
playersCharacter = player.Character
playersCharacter.Torso.CFrame = CFrame.new(Vector3.new(0, 203, 0))
end

script.Parent.MouseButton1Down:connect(Teleport)
```

Now test the script again. It works – great! Try scripting the BasePlate teleport button by yourself now. The script will look exactly the same, you will just need to change the y-position that you're moving the player to.

CHALLENGE

Try using the knowledge from this script-through and the last one to build a Teleporter that moves the player when they step on a brick.

Things to think about:
- How will you detect which player has stepped on the brick?
- What type of function will you need to use to do this?
- If you are making two Teleporters, one to move the player in one direction and another to teleport the player back, think about teleporting the player to be slightly off the teleporting bricks so that you don't get stuck teleporting back and forth really quickly.

TOOL GIVER
SCRIPT-THROUGH #3
INTRODUCTION TO SCRIPT-THROUGH

In this script-through, we will be learning how to make a tool which makes a player's Character invisible when they select it, then make a brick which can be stepped on to put the tool into the player's Backpack.

MAKING THE INVISIBILITY TOOL

First, we will be designing the invisibility tool itself. We are going to be making the tool as a "HopperBin" Object. This is an older but simpler method of making tools, and it's better to get to grips with making tools this way first. They are particularly useful for their "Selected" and "Deselected" events which occur when the tool is clicked in the player's Backpack.

We are going to be making our tool inside the "Lighting" folder. Putting items inside the Lighting folder doesn't affect the game in any way, so this folder can basically be used as a storage space for things that make up our game. The tool will sit in the Lighting folder until the player's Character steps on the tool-giving brick, at which point the tool will get cloned from the Lighting folder into the player's Backpack.

So let's get started:
    1.   Add a HopperBin Object as a child of Lighting. Name the HopperBin "Invisibility".

TOOL GIVER SCRIPT-THROUGH

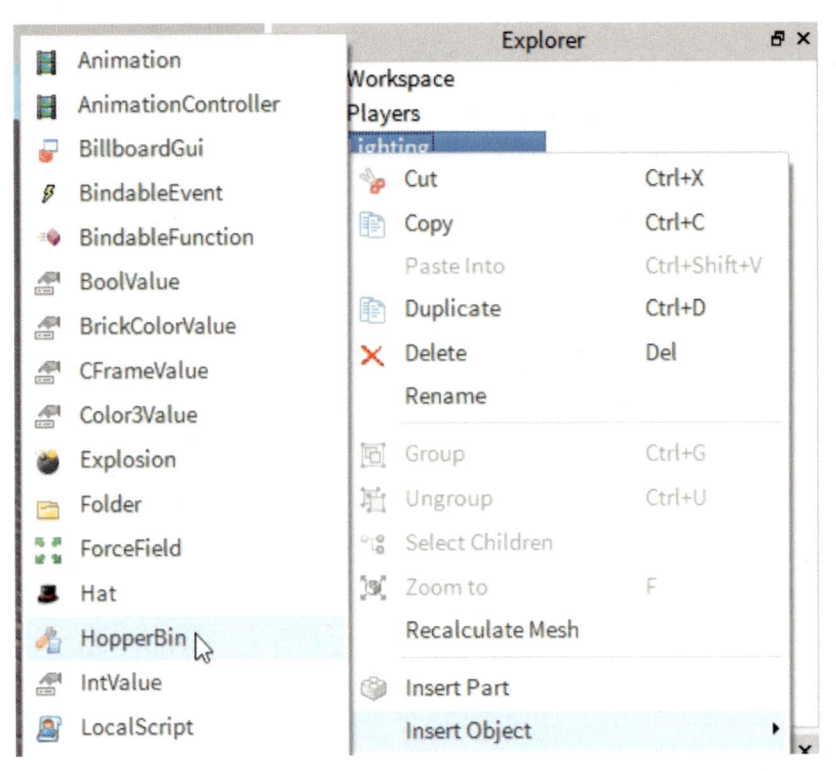

2. Add a LocalScript as a child of the HopperBin. We will use a LocalScript so that when the tool gets cloned into the player's Backpack, we can use "LocalPlayer" to find *that player* and make sure *that player* becomes invisible.

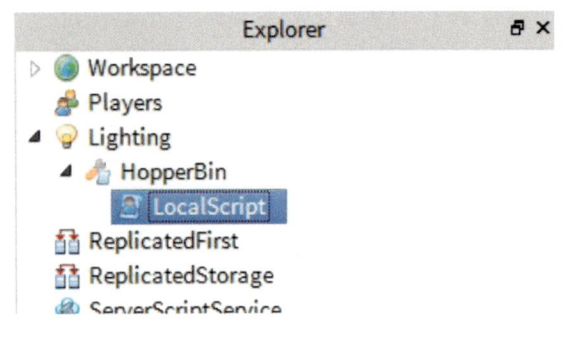

3. Now let's use our script to define the player and the player's Character:

```
player = game.Players.LocalPlayer
char = player.Character
```

4. Next we need to script both an "on" function for when the tool is selected that will make the player's Character invisible, and an "off" function for when the tool is deselected so that the player's Character becomes visible again. Let's start to type out our "on" function:

```
player = game.Players.LocalPlayer
char = player.Character

function on()
char.Torso.Transparency = 1
char.Head.Transparency = 1
end

script.Parent.Selected:connect(on)
```

We've begun to make some of the Character's parts invisible by setting their Transparency to 1, and written out the connection line using the Selected event. Let's make the rest of the Character invisible:

    5.   Write:

```
player = game.Players.LocalPlayer
char = player.Character

function on()
char.Torso.Transparency = 1
char.Head.Transparency = 1
char["Left Leg"].Transparency = 1
char["Right Leg"].Transparency = 1
char["Left Arm"].Transparency = 1
char["Right Arm"].Transparency = 1
end

script.Parent.Selected:connect(on)
```

We haven't come across the ["Name"] naming system before. Left Leg, Right Leg, etc are children of the Character Model but because they have a space in their name, we can't use "char.Left Leg" to change their transparency. Therefore, we use square brackets and quotation marks to define them without a full stop between "char" and "["Left Leg"]".

Now the next step is to add the "off" function for when the tool is deselected.

    6.   Write the new code:

TOOL GIVER SCRIPT-THROUGH

```
player = game.Players.LocalPlayer
char = player.Character

function on()
char.Torso.Transparency = 1
char.Head.Transparency = 1
char["Left Leg"].Transparency = 1
char["Right Leg"].Transparency = 1
char["Left Arm"].Transparency = 1
char["Right Arm"].Transparency = 1
end

function off()
char.Torso.Transparency = 0
char.Head.Transparency = 0
char["Left Leg"].Transparency = 0
char["Right Leg"].Transparency = 0
char["Left Arm"].Transparency = 0
char["Right Arm"].Transparency = 0
end

script.Parent.Selected:connect(on)
script.Parent.Deselected:connect(off)
```

To make the parts visible again we just set their transparency to 0. Add the new connection line for the Deselected event and the tool script is done.

NIFTY NUGGET: *If you want the player to have a tool when they start the game, just drop the tool into the StarterPack folder in Explorer.*

SCRIPTING THE GIVER BRICK

The next step is to make the brick which a player's Character must step on to be given the Invisibility tool:

    1.   Add a Part as a child of Workspace, then add a Script as a child of this Part. It's a good idea to make the Part fairly big and brightly colored so the player knows where to step. I've made mine 4x1x4 and Hot Pink in color.

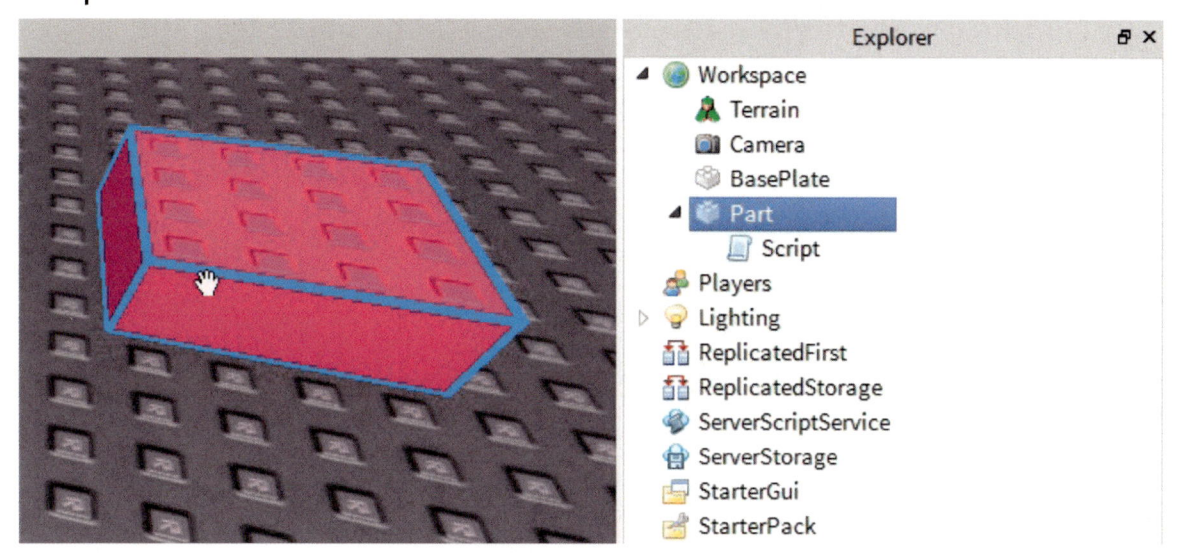

    2.   Go into the Script which is a child of Part. Here we will write the script which puts the Invisibility tool into the player's Backpack. First, we need to detect when the player steps onto the Part:

```lua
script.Parent.Touched:connect(function()
player = game:GetService("Players").LocalPlayer
end)
```

So we've used the GetService function and LocalPlayer to find out which player just stepped onto the Part so that player can be given the tool.

    3.   We only want to give the player the Invisibility tool if it's not already in their Backpack. To do this, we will use an if and then line which checks for the tool:

TOOL GIVER SCRIPT-THROUGH

69

```
script.Parent.Touched:connect(function()
player = game:GetService("Players").LocalPlayer
if player.Backpack:findFirstChild("Invisibility") == nil
then
end
end)
```

The script looks for "Invisibility" in the player's Backpack using the findFirstChild function. "== nil" is like saying "is not there". So this line is saying: **if** "Invisibility" is not in the players Backpack, **then** you can go to the next line.

> NIFTY NUGGET: You can use "~= nil" when you want to say "is not equal to nil" or "is there", or in this case by writing "~= nil" we would be saying "if the Invisibility tool IS in the player's Backapck". "~= nil" is like the opposite of "== nil".

4. The next thing we need to do is tell our script where it can find the Invisibility tool:

```
script.Parent.Touched:connect(function()
player = game:GetService("Players").LocalPlayer
if player.Backpack:findFirstChild("Invisibility") == nil
then
tool = game:GetService("Lighting").Invisibility
end
end)
```

Remember that in ROBLOX Studio, a Service is a folder in the Explorer. We need to use "GetService" to go into the Lighting folder and find the Invisibility tool.

5. The last step is to clone the tool from the Lighting folder into the player's Backpack:

```
script.Parent.Touched:connect(function()
player = game:GetService("Players").LocalPlayer
if player.Backpack:findFirstChild("Invisibility") == nil
then
tool = game:GetService("Lighting").Invisibility
tool:clone().Parent = player.Backpack
end
end)
```

That concludes this tutorial – test out the script!

WHAT NOW?

By now, you should understand well the basics of:
- How to use ROBLOX Studio.
- How to put a script together.
- How to write functions and events.
- How to use variables.
- How to use GUIs.

Those are just some examples. On top of that, there will be lots and lots of other pieces of information you will have picked up.

Scripting in ROBLOX Lua is full of exceptions and rules that you will simply need to learn and understand by **doing it** – (for example, moving a player by CFrame rather than Position in the teleporter tutorial). No matter how much you read and learn, you will probably never just know all of these little exceptions, and you will need to use other resources.

I've given you a good understanding of the major rules that will come up time and time again. All of the exceptions you'll run into on your own scripting journey will be variations of these rules. That doesn't mean you'll now be able to script everything completely by yourself. But, if you use the Internet and other resources, you've got a pretty good chance. I personally use the ROBLOX wiki all of the time for scripting, and the Scripting Helpers ROBLOX forum can be useful if you get stuck.

So now, if you want to make a tool, or a button that increases your player's Walkspeed, or a scripted trampoline, you know enough that you can think about it, see how other people have done it, learn from their script and then be able to do it yourself. Practise makes perfect, and the more you script, the better you'll get. Good luck on your scripting journey, and enjoy it – learning to script is great fun!

Made in the USA
Coppell, TX
12 November 2022